MONKEY BUSINESS

**FOR KAREN
AND OUR OWN LITTLE MONKEYS
BEN, SAM AND BECKY**

MONKEY BUSINESS

Why the way you manage is a million years out of date

by Gary Johnson

Gower

First published in hardback 1995 by Gower Publishing.

Paperback edition published 1997 by

Gower Publishing	Gower
Gower House	Old Post Road
Croft Road	Brookfield
Aldershot	Vermont 05036
Hants GU11 3HR	USA
England	

Gary Johnson has asserted his right under the Copyright, Designs and Patents Act 1988 to be identified as the author of this work.

British Library Cataloguing in Publication Data

Johnson, Gary
    Monkey Business
    I. Title
    658

ISBN 0–566–07620–9 Hardback
       0–566–08011–7 Paperback

Johnson, Gary, 1958–
    Monkey Business/Gary Johnson.
       P. CM.
    Includes bibliographical references and index.
    ISBN 0–566–07620–9
    1. Management. I. Title.
HD38.J615 1995
658—dc20

Typeset in Garamond by Raven Typesetters and printed in Great Britain by Biddles Ltd, Guildford.

CONTENTS

❖

PREFACE

❖

The world of management is a chaotic one. It's hard to see where fashion and fads end and fundamental truths begin. But there is a way. In the end, understanding management means understanding people. And people can appear quirky, illogical and downright bloody minded. The only way to really understand people is to understand the ultimate cause of human nature itself. And this, as you will come to appreciate, is rooted in our evolutionary past.

This is the first book for management to seize upon the enormous leaps in understanding the human condition that modern evolutionary science has given us. With this understanding, many of the 'inexplicable' events that surround managers suddenly become clear:

- O   what drives management fads and financial bubbles;
- O   why we are so often stressed at work and why this stifles our creativity;
- O   what motivates people:
  - makes them want to learn, to co-operate
  - makes them want to deceive, become aggressive;
- O   what makes some people leaders and others willing followers;
- O   what happens when two people communicate face to face.

Even more importantly, the understanding that follows is a highly practical one: it bears testing by a review of what happens in the real world and, most important of all, it can be acted upon in many ways to enhance your performance as a manager or business person.

It seems strange that this is the first attempt to apply the lessons of evolutionary biology to business and management. Particularly because, as you will see, it is in the 'business jungle' that our 'animal instincts' come to the fore, constantly whispering in the subconscious ear of the consumer, the venture capitalist, the chief executive under pressure, and nudging them all in the direction that millions of years of evolution would have them go. For, as Robert Heller (1989) has pointed out: 'Management is an arena for human behaviour at its most naked, under stress, but freed from many restraints of civilisation.' In retrospect the link will seem an obvious one.

But the acceptance of evolution first as a phenomenon and later as a force which explains present-day behaviour has been respectively slow and virtually non-existent. A hundred years ago at the time of Darwin people found it difficult or impossible to believe that a few thousand generations earlier their ancestors were hairy, ape-like creatures. Adam Sedgwick (1860), an eminent Victorian geologist, predicted that, if it accepted Darwin's ideas, humanity 'would suffer a damage that might brutalise it and sink the human race into a lower state of degradation than any to which it has fallen since written records tell us of its history'. He needn't have worried.

Today, it is true, most people accept evolution as a historical fact. But only as a *historical* fact: an interesting and bizarre piece of 'trivia' to file away with such trivia as who invented double-entry book keeping. Evolution plays no part in our view of life either for better or for worse.

It is amusing for us as business people to note that the creature that today presides over complex industries, travels on supersonic airliners and communicates via sophisticated information technology systems goes back in a direct parent and child line to a fish. But it is only amusing; it's not interesting or relevant. Our ape-like ancestors have been left far behind. Today we are civilized: products of our technology rather than our biology.

In fact, nothing could be further from the truth. Millions of business people are today slaves to the latest fashion. 'Diversify', cry the gurus, and they do. 'Stick to your knitting', cry the next generation of gurus, and they do. 'Buy', shout the financial pundits, and they do. 'Sell', shout those same pundits as the market crashes around them. If people would only look back a few decades, a few centuries, they would see the financial bubbles and the management fads come and go; they would develop a deeper appreciation of the realities of business. But to develop an understanding, not just an appreciation, of what is happening, they need to look back a great deal further; not just a few decades, or even a few centuries, but for many millennia. For it is there, in the mists of our evolutionary past, that the urges that drive these 'inexplicable' events arose.

So why is it that the study of evolution and the practice of management have followed totally divergent paths, with the profound lessons that the one has for the other going totally unobserved? I think that it is largely because they are at opposite ends of a social spectrum. The practice of business is the epitome of pragmatism. Its centres of excellence are the leading corporations of the day. Many of its practitioners eschew anything remotely academic and still consider the term 'business school' an oxymoron.

The study of evolution is high science. Its centres of excellence are the most prestigious universities, some of which (for example Oxford and Cambridge in the UK) are only now beginning to accept management as a subject worthy of academic study.

It is difficult to imagine anyone inhabiting either of these worlds seeing the relevance that the one has for the other. Yet, it did happen to me thanks to a couple of accidents of my particular history.

I am by profession a business man. However, my first degree was in medicine and while studying I developed an unusual hobby: sociobiology, the study of how our behaviour is explained by our evolution. Over the years my hobby and my profession started to overlap.

I practised business around the world and I was always warned and trained about the cultural differences that I would encounter. True enough, these differences exist and they are sometimes vast. But they are superficial. Once you get down to 'doing business', you are soon confronted by the same sort of animal: a self-centred business man or woman. I was continually struck by how often, as business people, we behave exactly how evolutionary theory says we should.

Years later, after a great deal of research, I am even more convinced of the truth in that original hypothesis and I am delighted by the practicality and usefulness of this approach to thinking about management. In the coming chapters you will learn a great deal about yourself and other people and about managing both of these. You will, for example, learn:

O   to reduce unproductive stress and its stranglehold on creativity;
O   why intuition is so often wrong and how to avoid the mistakes it can lead to;
O   why managers feel compelled to use unproven techniques like graphology and astrology – and to develop the confidence to ignore them yourself;
O   to lead effectively – rise above the deafening background noise of the workplace by tapping into people's power of concentration;
O   to avoid the sort of quality drives, rewards and incentive schemes and training programmes that do more harm than good. Understand people's real drives to really improve, teach and motivate them;
O   to avoid decisions that are too reckless or too safe and cosy by understanding how we assess and deal with risks;

○   what makes people aggressive and unco-operative so that you can structure an organization where effective teamwork flourishes;

○   to see through the instincts that lead to 'group think', 'yes men' so that you can foster original thought and free speech;

○   to make more rational decisions and relate better to people by managing the non-verbal cues that constitute most of our communication;

○   to stop being taken in. Understand why everyone is programmed for deceit. Learn how and where to look for it and how to detect it.

Each of the following chapters covers a particular aspect of human nature and shows how this manifests itself in business and management. Each chapter ends with a summary of what we have learnt and of what we can do about it.

These lessons, and indeed this book, are aimed at the 'thinking business person' – the sort of person who is interested in learning about the general nature of business and management, beyond the confines of the narrow specialism that they may currently work within. If you have read this far, we can assume that this applies to you. Because you care about your job, you may well be, like me, an avid reader of business books. You may also, like me, be disappointed by the way these books often marshal a collection of highly selected case studies to support the latest management fad. I have striven to provide you with something of a breath of fresh air. I have tried to produce a book that looks at the fundamentals of human nature and predicts best management practice, rather than a book that acts as a barometer for the latest management trends.

The book is necessarily aimed at the sort of person with a greater than average chance of reaching a senior management position (you may already be there). One of the few reliable indicators of what makes a good senior manager is the ability to take a 'helicopter view' of things – to see the big picture and to understand the driving forces behind a situation. Which is just what this book is trying to do as far as understanding people is concerned.

With that all said, no management book should over-promise. The world of management will always be a chaotic one. Every manager has to struggle constantly against data overload and the seemingly irrational behaviour of his or her colleagues and customers. We buy business books to make sense of that chaos and provide rules of thumb for making sensible decisions in the face of gnawing uncertainty. There are no panaceas. But I hope to have made a little more sense of it all by the time you finish this book.

Gary Johnson

1

STRESS
and how to stop it stifling creativity

❖

Because stress can be such a prominent feature of the management landscape, we will turn to it as our first example of how our evolution affects how we behave in business. We will see how our response to stress evolved to cope with vastly different circumstances to those we face as managers. And we will see that those responses are, therefore, completely inappropriate and counterproductive, stifling our creativity and damaging our health.

We are already aware of the need for managers to be more creative and there are a plethora of prescriptions; recall the 'lateral thinking' of Edward de Bono and the 'upside down thinking' from Charles Handy, and so on; their thesis is that, as a result of our experience and education, we tend to think in 'straight lines' and that we shouldn't. We should think more broadly (lateral thinking) and our thinking should encompass more unlikely possibilities and solutions (upside down thinking).

So why don't we? Writers have suggested various reasons. Scientific education, with its emphasis on causality, tends to foster straight line thinking. 'The establishment' that we find ourselves confronted with is always resistant to change or radical forms of thinking. We are conditioned and trained to act like the apocryphal generals who always insist on fighting yesterday's battles today. No doubt there's much truth in all this, but you'll notice that the blame is laid squarely at the door of our education, training and experience. Our biology escapes scot-free.

BIOLOGY IN THE DOCK

I'd like to suggest that our genes have a considerable influence on the way we think and an understanding of why will help us enormously. Consider a simple experiment conducted with a dog and a squirrel. The dog is placed several feet from an appetizing bowl of food. It is put on a leash. The leash runs away from the food, loops around a stake and then runs back to a post, next to the food, to which it is attached. To reach the food the dog simply has to walk away from the food, around the stake, thus unlooping the leash, and back towards the food; it is a simple detour problem. The dog will bark, whine, strain at the leash and eventually collapse exhausted but it's unlikely that it'll solve the problem.

Now take the supposedly less intelligent squirrel and set it the same test. Perhaps surprisingly it will quickly head away from the food, loop around the stake and run back to collect its prize. It seems hard to blame the dog's lack of 'lateral thinking' in this situation on its education.

Why should this happen? Think of the environment under which these animals' thought processes evolved. The dog is a ground dweller. The world it inhabits is essentially a flat, two-dimensional one. It sees something it wants and the most effective pattern of behaviour under these circumstances is to go directly towards it. It is prompted by its evolution to do just this in our experiment.

The squirrel on the other hand inhabits the more three-dimensional world of trees. Any inclination to charge straight for something it wanted would prove very unsuccessful. There may not be suitable branches to carry it on a direct route and such a route may lead the squirrel to leap into mid-air. This fatal behaviour pattern would be rapidly selected against. The squirrel has to be inclined constantly to consider indirect detours to arrive where it wants to be. It seems that it is this inborn ability that allows it to solve the problem in our experiment.

The dog is behaving in a wholly inappropriate fashion for the situation it finds itself in, because its evolution has programmed it to do so. Everyday business people behave in equally inappropriate ways for just the same reason. The main culprit is adrenalin.

THE TROUBLE WITH ADRENALIN

Adrenalin is the 'fight or flight' hormone. It evolved a long, long time ago for very good reasons. When our distant ancestors were faced with a stressful situation this normally constituted an immediate physical threat or opportunity: a sabre toothed tiger approaching, the proximity of game which might be caught or even an attractive member of the opposite sex.

Evolution selected those individuals best endowed for taking rapid advantage in such situations. This was achieved largely with the help of adrenalin.

Adrenalin prepares the body for fight of flight: it increases the heart rate and breathing rate to provide the muscles with the extra oxygen that they will require. It produces an emotional response: anxiety – you have to feel alarmed and disposed to do something about an approaching sabre toothed tiger. It prepares the brain which, under its influence, focuses its attention – obviously everything can wait until you're clear of the sabre toothed tiger – and solves problems very quickly. It's no good ruminating at length over the various options open to you as the sabre toothed tiger prepares to pounce. These are all clearly advantageous responses when a sudden short-term emergency arises and it's obvious why they evolved. In today's business environment, however, stressful situations tend to be of an altogether different nature.

First, they don't tend to be of a physical nature, and second, they don't tend to be of a sudden short-term nature. For example, this quarter's earnings are down. What is needed is some in-depth intellectual work: a careful examination of all the facts, all the options, their likely consequences and so on. Nothing physical, nothing sudden.

Unfortunately, however, the business person's body still recognizes this as a stressful situation: unless he does something he could lose his job and that constitutes a threat to his fitness. Any threat to his fitness provokes the non-specific stress response – bring out the adrenalin. With the adrenalin coursing around his veins, our business person is like the dog straining at the leash: abundant 'action' but little likelihood of it producing any positive result. In his state of anxiety he wants to 'do' something and his brain is sensitized to give him the fast decisions that he wants from his initial narrow perspective. Kenichi Ohmae in his classic *The Mind of the Strategist* (1982) describes just this phenomenon in business people:

> Business executives are no exception. The more severe the pressure, the more urgently a broader view is needed, the more dangerously their mental vision seems to narrow down.

Inevitably, our executive takes a fast decision and it is probably a poor decision. (Injecting someone with one part in a thousand adrenalin will significantly reduce his or her ability to do even simple mental arithmetic problems.) That makes the business situation worse; more stress; more adrenalin; more precipitous ill-considered decisions; the downward spiral couldn't be worse.

Yes it could. So far we've only considered the mental effects of adrenalin on decision making under these circumstances. Adrenalin was never meant to be produced day in day out for months on end and when it is, as a result of prolonged stress in business, the results can be appalling. It's hard to find a symptom that such stress cannot cause. Here are a few examples: tiredness, aches and pains, indigestion, migraine, impotence, palpitations, asthma, heart disease, arthritis, cancer. These are just some of the physical effects – and then there are the mental effects: irritability, anger, fear, guilt, paranoia, insomnia, hallucinations, alcohol and drug problems, phobias, psychoses – the list is endless.

These then are the effects that stress can have on an executive in the firing line. The fear of failure can lead the executive at best to poor, premature decision making and at worst, and all too often, to an early grave.

There may be those of a ruthless disposition who would argue that this culling by stress will soon select out those better capable to deal with it. There could be an awful truth in this and perhaps a hundred generations from now a population better equipped to survive long-term stress will actually have evolved! In the mean time there must be something that we can do.

Fortunately, there is an abundance of evidence as to which situations tend to cause most stress and in which situations stress does most harm. There are also many ways of acting upon this knowledge. We will look at all this next.

THINKING ABOUT WHAT SUCCESS MEANS

Most western business people bemoan short-termism. Short-termism can be a great unproductive stressor. It can take time to build results in many of today's more sophisticated business environments. Breathing down the necks of the managers of such organizations over every quarter's results produces stress which can ensure that carefully considered long-term plans that can produce long-term results are never produced. We often hear how the 'quarterly myopia' on Wall Street produces short-termism in management. Surely a component of this is that the resulting stress that this places on organizations prevents relaxed, in depth, long-term thinking.

In their book *Corporate Culture and Performance*, Professors John Kotter and James Heskett of Harvard Business School (1992), after analysing the culture and performance of many companies, concluded that firms whose cultures seem to produce consistent long-term success have one characteristic in common: they take a balanced view of the needs of all the firm's 'stakeholders' (employees, shareholders, suppliers, customers, etc.) and don't allow the short-term interests of shareholders to override everything else.

A constant short-term outlook can lead you into a vicious cycle. The stress produced leads to a failure to innovate and plan for the long term, which leads to declining performance, which leads to more stress, and so on.

It seems, not surprisingly, that it is much easier to avert this vicious cycle than to try and break it once it has been set in motion. Corporate turn-arounds are desperate situations and often require desperate, rapid and draconian measures – best to deal with these situations first, and then, once a company is on more of an even keel, try the more enlightened long-termist measures that are required for innovation and long-term survival. This is, not least, because the stress of a turn around is unlikely to be conducive to relaxed, creative thinking.

Graham Sharman, an expert in quality with McKinsey in Amsterdam, reckons that quality programmes work best if they are put in place *after* an ailing company has been turned around. 'Total quality is much easier to implement during a period of prosperity', he believes.

Another approach to thinking about success is to take a less desperate view of the need to 'succeed'. Kenichi Ohmae (1982) – President of McKinsey in Japan – suggests that,

> if the executive would try changing the objective from success at all costs to avoiding the worst, he would be sure to find a great many possible choices opening up.

This may be a different approach to thinking about business problems, but surely part of the wisdom stems from the fact that it is an entirely less stressful way of doing so.

THE FEAR OF FAILURE

It is possible to go one step further than Mr Ohmae suggests and, in some circumstances, consider removing the fear of failure all together.

One can't be too simplistic about this of course. If we didn't reward and advance those individuals capable of producing results we would never distil out the highly capable few that we need as our senior managers, our captains of industry. We are always looking for a compromise: one that identifies and advances talent but ameliorates the negative effects of a fear of failure.

Many companies have concluded that if they can't entirely remove the blow of failure, they can at least soften it. For example, the prospect of a sideways move into a staff job for unsuccessful line managers is far less fear inspiring than the prospect of the demise of their career.

Some companies have gone still one step further and made a virtue out of some forms of failure, not simply to relieve stress. Failure *can* be useful. Honda reckons that 90 per cent or so of its research projects fail first time. But the results are pooled and often used in future projects. This saves constant 'reinvention of the wheel' *and* removes some of the stigma and fear associated with failure.

Another way to remove the fear of failure is to allow executives to practise their thinking and synthesize new ideas in an environment other than their day-to-day jobs. One such approach is to recruit information technology in an attempt to excite executives into thinking in a broad, relaxed and creative way; many companies are encouraging executives to play with 'microworlds'. These are computer models of the firm and its market. By playing with computer models, where there is no penalty for failure, executives are brimming with ideas that would almost certainly have eluded them faced with the stresses of the 'real world'.

THINKING ABOUT ORGANIZATIONAL STRUCTURE

Perhaps *the* most popular management fad at the moment is to dismantle old, hierarchical organizational structures and replace them with 'flat' ones. This has arisen partly because information technology is eliminating the need for layers of administrators to process and filter information for senior managers. But also because hierarchical organizational structures stifle initiative and create fear and pressure. The inventor of scientific management, Frederick Taylor, summed it up when addressing Harvard students in 1909: 'your job is to find out what your boss wants and to give it to him exactly as he wants'. Not exactly conducive to free thought and innovation.

Hence companies across the globe are trying to establish 'flat', non-hierarchical structures or 'paper-weight' structures in Japan – in Japan paperweights are flat.

THINKING ABOUT MANAGEMENT STYLES

But, while the dash for flat organizations is undoubtedly a good thing in more situations than not, is it simplistic? Management is always situational. There are few if any generic truths. We have to think more deeply about the style we adopt.

We would expect that a management style that produces stress and thereby stifles creative, broad thinking would be particularly harmful in situations where creative, broad thinking is of vital importance. We would expect that such creative thinking is most needed in unstable, complex industries like computing and this is exactly what we find.

Kathlene Eisenhardt, a professor at Stanford, and Jay Bourgeois, a professor at the University of Virginia, made a detailed study of eight, small high-tech computer firms. They discovered that those firms with an 'authoritarian' management style found it hard to make strategic decisions. (They were also the poorest performers as they failed to react swiftly and thoughtfully to the rapid changes in their markets.)

Indeed, this does seem to be a general truth. More complex management environments require a lighter, less stressful approach to management.

Michael Goold and Andrew Campbell, in their seminal work *Strategies and Styles* (1990), noted that the style of corporate management that produced the best results in such complex industries was one that emphasized strategic thinking and goals and played down control, particularly tight financial control. They concluded that such a style

> is most suitable for businesses that have close links with other units, where the decisions are large and have long payback periods, and where the competitive environment is unstable, either because the market place is wide open or because the companies are caught in a fierce battle.

In other words a less highly pressured and long-term environment is best where broad thinking is required.

On the other hand Goold and Campbell noted that the style that produced the best results in less complex industries *was* a style of tight, short-term financial control. As Goold and Campbell concluded (ibid), this style

> is likely to bring out the best where there are few linkages, where investments are small and the money can be recovered in 2 or 3 years, and where the competitors are not overly aggressive.

In other words high pressure is effective when the environment is so simple that broad, free thinking is not really required.

A similar pattern emerges if you look at the style of management adopted for R&D and the sort of innovations that are produced. Product innovation is a delicate flower indeed and hard-headed commercial managers seldom have 'green fingers' as far as it is concerned. It is easy to show that even moderate amounts of stress stifle innovative thinking in an experimental setting.

For example, in one study two groups of subjects were set a conundrum (S. Glucksberg 1962). They were given a candle, a cigarette lighter and a box of tacks and asked how they would use these to attach the candle to the wall. The answer requires a degree of lateral thinking in that you have to discard the tacks, use molten wax to attach the box to the wall and then stand the candle on it. So, you have to be innovative enough to see the box fulfilling a different role – that of a platform – to that intended for it. The difference between the two groups was that one was offered a reward for solving the problem whereas the other wasn't. The prospect of a reward looming in the mind is a stressor and prevents flexibility of thought. Sure enough, the group who were offered the reward took three and a half minutes longer to solve the problem.

There is also evidence that, away from the psychologist's lab, stress has the same sort of effect on innovation in business. If people are tightly focused and put under commercial stress, they tend only to be able to develop ideas for small ('incremental') innovations and not the 'quantum leap' variety that requires relaxed lateral thinking.

For example *The Economist* (13 April 1991) reviewed the global management of R&D and concluded that:

> All this, however, leaves firms with a dilemma. If R&D concentrates on research that is more closely integrated with the firm's overall strategy, the department's ability to churn out incremental developments of existing products will almost certainly improve – which can help the company stay one step ahead of its rivals. But the trade – off may be that the chance of the company producing an off-beat blockbuster will be greatly reduced - commercial realities tend to stifle innovation.

Therefore a look at the effects of pressure on R&D has delivered the same conclusion as for management in general: pressure is effective when the environment is so simple that broad, free thinking is not really required.

HOW MANY BUSINESSES CAN SURVIVE WITHOUT RELAXED, CREATIVE THINKING?

The question that then has to be asked, however, is just how many environments are likely to stay that simple for very long? If we take a particularly long-term view, the answer seems to be that companies can't survive over the long haul merely on the small, incremental innovations that high pressure management produces. They need periodic infusions of *real* innovation.

Arie de Geus, when he was Chief Planning Strategist at Royal Dutch/ Shell, surveyed that rare animal the geriatric corporation. Of the very few companies that had survived 75 years or more (without going bust or being swallowed up) the key characteristic appeared to be an ability to run 'experiments on the margin': to encourage off-beat experimentation and produce breakthrough innovation.

While this need for pure innovation held true in the past, it has to be even truer for the future. Management today is increasingly a fast paced 'mind game'. Business problems become ever more complex as markets globalize and product life-cycles shrink. In the days when product life-cycles were much longer than they are today, just keeping up with the competition could prove a viable strategy for a time. Alfred Sloan (1967), the founder of General Motors, exemplifies this in his statement that:

> It was not necessary to lead in technical design or run the risk of untried experiments, provided that our cars were at least equal in design to the best of our competitors' in a grade.

But the world has changed – and GM's recent problems testify to this!

Innovation and speedy response to the market is becoming necessary even in seemingly stable industries. The average model life of a Japanese car is now four years and falling, while that of a European car is 12 years. Japanese car makers produce the tools and dies that make their cars in a fifth of the time that their European rivals do.

Major innovation is occurring in once stable industries and not just in the products themselves, but even in the way the products are designed and manufactured.

WHAT NOT TO DO

We can conclude that there is a need for at least some relaxed, creative thinking in most industries – for some, like computing, for short-term survival, for most others at least for long-term survival. We can now look at some of the current management obsessions that won't deliver this.

One of the current management buzzwords is 'benchmarking' – matching the best practice of your competitors. Many western companies are facing up to the Japanese threat by trying to ape (belatedly) techniques already developed and operating in Japan (like just-in-time stock control, quality circles and more recent Japanese innovations like concurrent engineering where parts of a product are developed in parallel by different teams, rather than one after another, to reduce development times still further). The trouble with this fad is that it is Alfred P. Sloan's approach re-visited. To be sure, a firm has to match the best practices of its competition but only as a base to build on. It is a *sine qua non*; it is axiomatic but, as we have seen, it is not enough by itself.

Further, a failure to innovate will lead to a corporate downturn and that tends to elicit the ultimate in reflex management: 'downsizing'. This is the charming buzzword-come-euphemism for closing plants, removing layers of managers and subcontracting out or discontinuing areas of activity. In other words sacking large numbers of people. Invariably management justifies the mass redundancies as being necessary to secure the future for the remaining employees. Unfortunately, the sacrifices seldom seem to work.

In 1992 Right Associates, a Philadelphia-based consultancy, polled over a thousand US companies, over three-quarters of whom said they had 'downsized' in the last five years. Of these about a third had sacked over 500 people. Three-quarters of the firms that had downsized said that their financial performance had not improved as a result. Two-thirds said that they had not seen any improvement in productivity.

The main reason seems to be that the downsizing is not accompanied by any strategic thinking. Perhaps this is inevitable given that managers will necessarily be forced to downsize during times of maximum stress, when performance is poor and their own necks are on the block.

The Right survey seems to confirm this. Less than half the firms who downsized saw their moves as part of a broader overhaul. They just espoused platitudes about becoming 'more competitive'. The result of this (stress induced) failure to think strategically is that downsizing firms are likely merely to become smaller firms with the same problems. Corporate history, unfortunately, bears this out. By far the most reliable predictor of whether a firm will downsize in the future is whether it has downsized in its recent past.

We have seen, then, that any form of management by fear where creative intellectual work is involved is likely to be counterproductive and that there are many tried and tested techniques for fostering relaxed, creative thought. This message has been delivered time and time again by enlightened management commentators. An alarming number of companies have still to understand this message – hopefully a look at the biology of stress will enlighten one or two more.

STRESS FURTHER DOWN THE ORGANIZATION

So far we considered the effects of stress on senior managers, charged with producing results for their organizations. The pressures these people are under seem unenviable. You'd assume that for those sheltered from having to make similarly monumental decisions the stress suffered wouldn't be nearly so great. Unfortunately you'd be wrong.

The effects of not being able to make the decisions that shape your destiny can be far worse than making them. Consider the fate of the two rats in this fascinating experiment (N. Dixon 1988). The rats are placed in separate cages and wired so that an unpleasant electric shock can be administered at random intervals to their tails. The first rat has a light in its cage which shines just before each shock is given. Its cage also contains a lever which, if pushed, will prevent the shock being administered to itself and also to the second rat. It soon learns to push the lever when it sees the light but occasionally laziness prevails and it fails to push the lever and receives an unpleasant shock. Nevertheless its fate is in its own hands, or rather paws. The rat takes the decisions which control its own destiny. It is an executive rat.

The second rat has no light and no lever. All it is given are the shocks every time the first rat decides not to push its lever. It receives exactly the same shocks as the first rat, but whether the shock comes or not is out of its control. This rat is helpless. It is a subordinate rat.

The rats were killed after the experiment had been running for some time, and post-mortems performed. The first rat, the executive rat, is in fine shape (apart from the fact that it is dead). The second rat has been ravaged by all the signs of stress-related disease (you recall that fearful list of them earlier this chapter).

It is not the electric shocks that have so stressed this poor rat – the executive rat suffered exactly the same shocks – it is the state of helplessness. Being unable to control its destiny is an obvious threat to the fitness of an animal and again it is the non-specific stress response – adrenalin, constant unremitting adrenalin – which causes the damage.

Again, we can't prove that 'helplessness' causes the same potentially lethal stress levels in humans by conducting exactly the same experiment as we did with the rats. But unfortunately many businesses still provide almost identical conditions to those suffered by our subordinate rat with the result that the health of the subordinate humans suffers in exactly the same way.

The famous 'Whitehall Study' (1991) looked at stress-related disease in British civil servants. As you would expect, it was not the executives who suffered the worst stress, it was their underlings: the poor unfortunates, chained to their in-trays with no one to delegate to and no authority. Their 'electric shocks' are a constant inflow of work beyond their capacity to perform in terms of volume and their authority to deal with it.

Studies into the mental health of workers repeatedly show that it is a lack of the factors which give workers control over their destinies that causes stress-related problems: a lack of feedback about the results of their work (aleviation of this stressor is even being 'built into' modern computer systems – if workers aren't told about the state of the system after each input they begin to feel helpless); lack of information about the company's future plans and the career path for the worker; a lack of clear information about the type and standards of behaviour expected in a job; a lack of variety; unmanageably high volumes of work; stultifyingly low volumes of work or an inability for the worker to use his or her skills and training.

Time and time again these factors have been shown to produce stress and its attendant problems. Isn't it tragic then that time and time again it has been shown that responsibility is the greatest motivator in business. Depriving people of responsibility begins to look like a sin doesn't it; it kills productivity and kills people. To the Catholic Church it *is* a sin. The Catholic Church upholds a concept known as 'subsidiarity'. To quote Charles Handy (1989):

> It is a word unfamiliar to most [this was written pre-Maastricht!], but not to the adherents of the Roman Catholic Church where it has long been an established part of traditional doctrine. First enunciated by Pope Leo X, but later recalled in the papal encyclical 'Quadragesimo Anno' in 1947 at the time of Mussolini, the principle of subsidiarity holds that 'it is an injustice, a grave evil and a disturbance of right order for a large and higher organisation to arrogate to itself functions which can be performed efficiently by smaller and lower bodies'. To steal other people's decisions is wrong.

IN CONCLUSION

The central theme of this chapter – that too much stress is bad news in the modern business environment – doesn't find favour with a great many managers. You'll recognize them by their maxims which glorify all things unpleasant and stressful: 'no pain no gain'; 'I came up the hard way'.

Such attitudes are of course grounded in the military management model which was adopted by the early industrialists. Management by fear and coercion may be quite effective when you need to motivate a body of men to charge into a hail of bullets – in fact it's difficult to see how else you could achieve this. Management by fear also proved effective for the early industrialists who required their workers to perform soul-destroyingly monotonous mass production jobs unquestioningly. Again it's hard to see any other form of management working -no one would embark on such work out of love for the job.

But the world has changed. Only thirty years ago over half the workers in developed countries were involved in making things. Now about a fifth of them are. Increasingly working means thinking. Most workers are what Peter Drucker has labelled 'knowledge workers', and fear-centred, military management models have become irrelevant history for them.

IN SUMMARY

WHAT HAVE WE LEARNT?

Most business people think that evolution is an irrelevance. They are wrong. The forces driving many of the 'inexplicable' events that surround them would become crystal clear if they considered their evolution. An outstanding example of this can be found in our response to stress.

Our body's general response to stress involves the release of adrenalin, the 'fight or flight' hormone. It evolved a long, long time ago. Then, a stressful situation tended to be some immediate physical threat – like an approaching sabre toothed tiger. So, the response that adrenalin elicits evolved to deal with this sort of threat. Physically, your heart rate and breathing increase to give your muscles the extra oxygen they need for 'fight or flight'. Mentally, your brain's attention narrows; it focuses on the immediate problem and it is primed for fast decision taking and fast action. All of which is great for dealing with a sabre toothed tiger, but disastrous for decision making in business.

(Also, sabre toothed tiger scares tended to be short-lived affairs – a burst of adrenalin was a life saver. Business stress tends to be long term – and unrelenting adrenalin is a killer.)

There are many familiar causes of (often unnecessary) stress in business: an obsession with short-term results; neglecting to make plans and take action until a crisis looms; an obsession with 'success at all costs' and the fear of failure that this generates; and hierarchical, dictatorial management structures.

Such stressors – and the lack of creative thinking and the innovation that they can induce – are proven causes of corporate failure. Furthermore, while companies in fast-moving, highly competitive environments tend to fail rather quickly if they don't innovate, even companies in stable, 'safe' industries will eventually succumb if they don't calm down and *think* at least some of the time.

WHAT CAN WE DO ABOUT IT?

○ Don't succumb to short-termism. Resist the 'quarterly myopia' of thinking only of your shareholders' reaction to your latest profits statement. Take a balanced view of the long- and short-term needs of your company and of its stakeholders (shareholders, employees, suppliers, customers and so on).

○ Don't wait for a crisis before you take action. Many business people feel most valuable during a crisis. Genuine value and long-term prosperity comes from the sort of innovation that is unlikely to stem from fire fighting.

○ Don't let the fear of failure stifle your organization. Consider sideways moves rather than dismissals when executives fail. Recognize that failures – and the lessons learned – can be useful. Let your executives practise thinking 'off-line' in simulated environments where mistakes won't damage the company. Do away with critical, hierarchical management systems.

○ Make sure that, even in simple industries, some people are allowed to think in a relaxed and innovative way. (They won't be employed in high pressure, line jobs!)

○ Don't believe that reactive management techniques such as benchmarking and downsizing are enough in themselves for long-term survival. Necessary as they may be, they have to be accompanied by creativity and innovation.

2

LIFE
and how it got here

❖

We have seen, through our exploration of stress, one way in which our evolution affects our behaviour as managers. And an understanding of the biology of stress is vital because stress is such a constant threat to our effectiveness as managers. But, important as it may be, our response to stress is just one of the myriad ways in which evolution shapes our thoughts and actions. Furthermore, while our response to stress is a blatant demonstration of our biology's influence on our behaviour (which is why we started with it), many other effects are more subtle and more elusive. To begin to understand the richness of this influence, therefore, it is now necessary to take a step back; to appreciate how profoundly our biology affects our behaviour and to understand the force that has caused this, evolution.

HOW MUCH DOES OUR BIOLOGY AFFECT OUR BEHAVIOUR?

Simone de Beauvoir described humans as '*l'être dont l'être est de n'être pas*' – the being whose essence is having no essence; we humans are, as many social scientists would have it, a '*tabula rasa*', a 'blank slate', upon which the hand of experience and learning writes; we are devoid of any 'instincts' of significance. Industrialization did much to foster this notion. Mass production with its militaristic management methods successfully treated workers as programmable machines and workers, by and large, had to fall in line. A typical business person's education, training and experience, which is still largely rooted in this tradition, will do much to reinforce the notion.

However, the fact that brutal management methods and fear can dehumanize people and turn them into highly predictable androids does not mean that they do not possess a rich and subtle set of instincts. In fact by understanding these we can actually get far more from our people than we can by merely squashing them. But before we can even begin to consider how, we must first rid ourselves of the notion that biology has no important influence on human behaviour. As some people find this a difficult concept to accept we'll edge our way in slowly.

Now the fact that animals have instincts and that their behaviour is largely determined by these instincts is widely acknowledged. People find it easy to accept that the bird singing, the kitten pawing at anything that moves and the dog cocking its leg are acting on instinct. But these are not intellectual behaviours and so it is difficult to link these with the sorts of complex behaviours humans exhibit in the modern world.

We must, therefore, look at animals performing a more 'human' activity – rats learning to find their way through a maze. It's harder to see instinct or biology playing a role here. And yet if you take a group of rats, test them on a maze, breed the brightest rats together and the dullest rats together and continue this procedure for a few generations, you soon have two populations of rats with vastly differing abilities to find their way around mazes. Hence an animal's behaviour can be influenced by evolution (which is exactly what you have just witnessed) very markedly and very quickly.

Can the same be true of humans? Well it's hard to set up an experiment like the rat one with people involved but, fortunately, other sorts of evidence abound. First, consider your own experience. Indeed consider your very first experience – as a newborn baby instinctively crying and suckling. So it is relatively easy to accept that humans have some instincts but not necessarily where the sort of complex intellectual activities seen in business are concerned. In fact this book will be concerned with something far more subtle than instinct. Instinct is a pre-programmed pattern of behaviour, such as suckling. We shall be looking at inclinations, tendencies, capabilities. We shall be seeing not how we are pre-programmed in everything we do like biological androids, but how at important junctures our biology can tip the balance in the direction that millions of years of evolution suggest.

Let's take, for example, talking. But isn't talking entirely a learnt activity? Well yes, but try teaching our friends the rats (even the expert maze negotiators that we bred) to talk. Think about it. Humans have an inborn ability to learn speech and rats don't. At the simplest level humans have evolved large brains which allow them to master speech and rats have evolved small brains that don't. The ability of a child to master the complexity and abstractions of speech so quickly is due not simply to a large brain but to a highly specialized area of the brain – the speech centre – which confers the ability to learn speech. A human child does not have to be 'taught' speech; he or she will pick it up because of the innate ability that the speech centre confers. There is even an instinct for basic grammar; in one study deaf children who had no experience of formal sign language spontaneously developed their own system which contained many of the grammatical properties of conventional spoken language. And all human languages, even for remote tribes who have lived in isolation from other humans for millennia, have the same grammatical units in common. Remove the speech centre from a child and despite the vast amount of brain remaining (most of which is surplus capacity) the child will not be able to master speech.

If an inborn propensity to learn or even develop such a complex task as speech has evolved, it now begins to look reasonable that many other aspects of behaviour could also be so influenced.

Still you may not be convinced. After all we have talked about one special evolved ability – speech – and while it's hard to imagine business without such an ability, the ability does not in any way predispose how we should use it – how we should make, for example, business decisions.

Let's elaborate further with a particularly elegant demonstration of how we can inherit certain behaviour traits and reflect on identical twins. If behaviour traits are inherited, identical twins should show unusually similar personalities. This is exactly what we find.

Ah, you might (rightly) say, but identical twins will have similar environments. Couldn't it be this producing the similarities? Well, fortunately, there is another type of twins – non-identical twins – who, despite being exposed to the same domestic environment, don't show anything like the similarities of identical twins. Then there are the identical twins separated at birth (as when they are orphaned) and brought up in completely separate environments with no communication between them. The first meeting of two such identical twins was eerily described by T. J. Bouchard (1984):

> Their families had never corresponded, yet similarities were evident when they first met at the airport. Both sported moustaches, and two pocket shirts with epaulettes. Each had his wire-rimmed glasses with him. They share abundant idiosyncrasies. The twins like spicy foods and sweet liquors, are absent minded, fall asleep in front of the television, think it is funny to sneeze in a crowd of strangers, flush the toilet before using it, store rubber bands on their wrists, read magazines from back to front, and dip buttered toast in their coffee.

In fact researchers have now shown that there are countless behavioural tendencies which can be inherited to a greater or lesser extent. For example: introversion–extroversion measures, personal tempo, psychomotor and sports activities, neuroticism, dominance, depression, age of first sexual activity, timing of significant cognitive development and the tendency toward certain forms of mental illness such as schizophrenia, locomotion, posture, muscular tone and emotional response to newborn infants.

I hope by now that you are sufficiently convinced that we can inherit certain behavioural traits. Or if not, that you can suspend your disbelief while you read the rest of this book, by which time, I guarantee, you *will* be convinced. I have demonstrated that we can inherit behavioural traits essentially by showing that there are differences in behaviour between individuals (and species) and that these different behavioural traits can be passed on to (or inherited by) offspring. Incidentally, these are the necessary conditions for evolution to occur (as we shall see later) but from now on we will not be so concerned with differences as with similarities. We shall be identifying the key inborn behavioural tendencies of people, seeing and understanding why, from an evolutionary point of view, these arose and discussing their role and importance in the modern business environment.

First, however, we must acquire a basic understanding of evolution. You will not require any knowledge of the complex biochemistry or mathematics involved, just the basic concepts. And so here, for the busy business person, is a précis, an executive summary if you like, of all that you will need to know about evolution.

SURVIVAL OF THE FITTEST

As I said at the outset of Chapter 1, evolution is for most people a curiosity; so much so that most people's understanding is based on a number of folk tales which have survived because of their interest value and their appeal to common sense but which are, nevertheless, hopelessly wrong. This account of evolution will therefore consist mainly of correcting these preconceptions.

Now everyone knows that Darwin discovered evolution. Right? Wrong. And so we tackle the first of our preconceptions. The idea that living things evolved from a common ancestor was suggested long before Darwin. Darwin's contribution was to propose a mechanism by which evolution could take place: the theory of Natural Selection. Interestingly Darwin developed his theory by applying Adam Smith's *laissez-faire* economic models to biology and, as the idea originally came from the world of economics/business, it is about time that the business community understood it and took advantage of the amazing insights that an understanding can provide.

Darwin's theory was one of those that is so obvious to us now that it's difficult to imagine the controversy and resistance that it provoked. It stems from three observations. The first is this. The potential reproductive power of animals and plants is unlimited. In a population of rabbits, for example, (it could just as easily be any other animal but the concept of reproductive potential sits well with the rabbit) if left unchecked, each rabbit would have ten offspring (and unchecked they'd do vastly better than this). Each generation is one year, therefore in 23 years there would be more rabbits than there are atoms in the known universe. Were this not impossible the same state of affairs would be reached (at differing times) by any other species of plant or animal left to breed unchecked. While rabbits do reproduce at this sort of rate, the reason that we are not all submerged in a heaving mass of them is that the offspring are constantly culled by lack of food, predators, disease and man's activities. Only a small proportion of rabbit young achieve reproductive maturity.

The second observation is that there is variation among offspring. The third is that offspring tend to resemble their parents – not exactly or that would belie the second observation, but offspring will tend to be more similar to their parents than are offspring of other parents.

These then are the conditions for 'Darwinian' evolution. The offspring which are most cleverly adapted to deal with the shortage of food, predators, disease and so on will tend to survive and reproduce and the resulting offspring will tend to inherit the adaptations.

NATURE RED IN TOOTH AND CLAW

This mechanism may well ring a bell: 'survival of the fittest'. In this context fitness simply means reproductive success – an individual's success in producing offspring who survive to have offspring of their own.

But people have insisted in reading values, even morals, into evolution. This is nonsense; evolution is neither good nor bad; it just 'is'. Nevertheless people see a grand design in evolution: a mechanism whose 'purpose' was to produce more and more sophisticated and complicated organisms, culminating with us. We talk of 'higher' and 'lower' animals as though, because our own fitness-maximizing strategy has been to develop a sophisticated brain, there is something 'better' about this particular approach to surviving. Darwin himself made notes to remind himself not to use these terms. Evolution does not reward sophistication in an organism, just fitness: blindly and ruthlessly.

Nearly a quarter of animal species are beetles. A group of clergymen once asked J.B.S. Haldane, a great British evolutionary biologist, what a lifetime's study of evolution had taught him about the nature of God, to which he responded, 'An inordinate fondness of beetles'.

Particularly inappropriate and pernicious value judgements have been applied to the 'survival of the fittest' concept. Fitness was, and often still is, equated with violence and selfishness, Tennyson's 'nature red in tooth and claw' summing most people's understanding.

I said earlier that business people have never understood and applied the lessons of evolution. Unfortunately that is not to say that they have never misunderstood and misapplied them. Towards the latter half of the nineteenth century natural selection was becoming more and more widely accepted and (mis)understood. This was a time when capitalism in the western world was unchallenged and the idea that evolution was a life and death struggle where the 'strong' survived and the 'weak' went to the wall was a perfect rationalization for some of the extreme social inequalities of the time. This view was even known as 'Social Darwinism' and many a mill owner justified his appalling working conditions in this way.

And conditions were mind-numbingly appalling. Children began work as young as four years old, working up to a 16-hour day. They could perform the same repetitive task on a machine for so long that their little bodies became deformed. An experienced mill worker knew which machine a child operated by its deformity.

Why then were the Social Darwinists wrong? As we have seen, fitness, more accurately, means reproductive success – it is measured by the number of offspring who survive to have offspring of their own and this can arise just as easily from greater co-operation and altruism as it can from violence and subjugation. Indeed if the mistreated working classes were having more children they were arguably 'fitter' than their oppressors. 'Fitness' should carry no particular values or assumptions. That didn't stop the Social Darwinists and it hasn't stopped racists, sexists, nepotists and others using evolution and natural selection to justify their cause.

This is not, however, the only example of the world of commerce entering into a regrettable involvement with the concept of evolution. While the Social Darwinists at the turn of the century had eagerly embraced Darwinism as a 'justification' for *laissez-faire* capitalism, the Soviet Union, between 1930 and 1960, had the opposite problem. Any theory which read like a biological recipe for unchecked capitalism was a threat to their credo of Communism and had to be rejected; they rewrote evolution and imprisoned their geneticists.

What the Soviets chose to believe is called Lamarckism. This is a highly plausible explanation which appeals to common sense and is a widely held misconception even today. It runs like this. Evolutionary change is produced by the effects of the environment *during the lifetime* of an organism and, once acquired, these changes can be passed on to the next generation. A Lamarckian explanation of the giraffe's long neck would involve early short-necked giraffes spending a lifetime reaching up for leaves and stretching their necks slightly in the process. The next generation inherits this feature and is born with a slightly longer neck and so on. This has socialist appeal – the giraffe has evolved his long neck through his own efforts and this has a far more satisfying parallel with a centrally planned economy.

In a sense it is unfortunate that this was not mere propaganda. The

Soviets practised what they preached. In an effort to breed wheat which would withstand their winter they exposed seedlings to cold, allowed them to mature and seed, grew a new generation of seedlings, exposed them to cold and so on. Each generation of seedlings, it was believed, would develop a slightly greater resistance to the cold and this would be passed on to the next generation in a cumulative fashion.

Of course this programme proved as disastrously unproductive for the Soviets as did the central planning of their overall economy that they so wanted their model of evolution to parallel, and it played havoc with the agricultural sector of their economy for many years.

Both the Social Darwinists and the Russians misapplied evolution because of misunderstandings. Other misapplications are based on a less flawed understanding. There may well be a defensible argument for evolution favouring nepotism (as we shall see later). But the idea that because something is natural it is good or right simply doesn't hold. As Ogden Nash once said, 'Smallpox is natural, vaccine ain't'.

Ninety-nine per cent of our evolution took place during a period when we did not have access to the products of our technology. Our capacity for conflict and aggression undoubtedly made good evolutionary sense during our pre-history when it developed. Then we only had sticks and stones at our disposal. Unfortunately the same instincts, applied to the use of nuclear weapons, could prove cataclysmically inappropriate. The instincts which once served us so well could, quite conceivably, destroy us. Still in a sense we can't complain. Without our aggressive tendencies we would never have survived to be faced with the dilemma and the paradox.

An awareness of evolution does not require a fatalistic surrender to our biology. Indeed the survival of our species may well depend on our developing a better understanding of and control over our natures. This may sound a little melodramatic for a business book, but with the power of multinationals to consume the world's rain forests, pollute the oceans, service arms races, etc., etc., a note of sobriety is in order.

THE ORIGINS OF LIFE

How life began remains conjecture. Sometime, somehow, somewhere during the unimaginably long history of the earth, in the unimaginably vast volumes of all the oceans and lands of the earth an unimaginably unlikely occurrence happened: a molecule arose with the ability to take the ingredients in its environment (probably the 'pre-biotic soup' of the primordial oceans: a rich source of amino acids, the building blocks of life, created by the action of lightning in a simple methane and ammonia atmosphere) and make copies of itself.

As the self-replicating molecule reproduced there were occasional errors and the resulting 'offspring' differed from the original. Usually the errors would have been harmful (as is the case with errors) but occasionally they conferred an advantage – possibly allowing, for example, faster reproduction. Such self-replicating molecules would be at an advantage over the others and would come to dominate the population – 'survival of the fittest'. The evolution that would eventually lead to you and me had begun.

The variation that has allowed the whole of evolution was produced by these errors of replication or 'mutations'. Mutations tend to be small (not the drastic type producing the bug-eyed monsters out of humans in science fiction – another misconception) and infrequent (as most of them are harmful life could not survive otherwise). Furthermore evolution does not select the best possible way of achieving something (another popular misconception), merely the best alternative offered by the mutations that occur. Often the two are not at all the same.

Then at some time during the unimaginably long history of these self-replicating molecules an unimaginably unlikely mutation occurred which allowed the self-replicating molecule to use some of the materials in its environment for means other than to produce copies of itself – possibly to produce another sort of chemical – a protein – which could chemically break down other self-replicating molecules and so use their components to make copies of itself: as food.

Then molecules of DNA learned to do more than one trick: different parts of the DNA molecule produced different types of protein each of which could do a different trick or fulfil a different function. Each of these different lengths of DNA is called a gene. Perhaps, for example, one gene produced a protein to break down one part of other replicators while another gene produced a different protein to break down another part. Then some genes learned to construct proteins which manufactured a protective capsule around the DNA to produce the first cells. The first cells were produced some 3.5 billion years ago and life proceeded much the same until about 800 million years ago. Then some cells (or more properly the DNA inside them) learned that when they replicated, instead of the two cells always going their separate ways, there were advantages in two or more cells sticking together with different groups of cells performing different roles. These were the first organisms or 'organizations of cells'.

Before our story can continue we need to stop and think about what is actually happening. Bear in mind that however elaborate these organisms became (culminating as they did with animals such as ourselves; phenomenally intricate machines comprised of over one hundred million cells) they came about only because they increased the fitness of the self-replicating molecules of DNA nestling inside each cell. Richard Dawkins (1976) the great elucidator of evolution puts it like this:

We are all survival machines for the same kind of replicator – molecules called DNA – but there are many different ways of making a living in the world, and the replicators have built a vast range of machines to exploit them. A monkey is a machine which preserves genes up a tree, a fish is a machine which preserves genes in the water; there is even a small worm which preserves genes in German beer mats. DNA works in mysterious ways.

Even today almost everything DNA achieves – like building the complex body you're sitting in and running all the chemical reactions going on inside it – it achieves just by building proteins. Apart from making copies of itself this is really the only other trick it's learned to do through the aeons.

Perhaps that's not quite true. The other trick it had to invent, you'll be pleased to hear, was sex, and, you may be less pleased to hear, a necessary 'part' of sex, as we shall see, was death.

About 900 million years ago organisms (or more correctly the genes within them), again no doubt by some incomprehensibly unlikely accident, learned that they could increase their fitness by, instead of making exact copies of themselves, trading genes with other similar organisms. This was sexual reproduction and it proved staggeringly successful. The reason that sex was so successful was that now a mutation which conferred a survival advantage to an organism could be rapidly acquired by the offspring of all the organisms who participated in the gene trading arrangement (and this is what we call a species). Now instead of each organism having to wait the impossibly long times required to experience each possible beneficial mutation itself (and probably become extinct during the wait) it could acquire these for its offspring very quickly.

In order to take full advantage of this phenomenon, it was necessary for the genes to invent death. That is not to say that individual organisms prior to sexual reproduction did not die. They did, but as every replication produced an identical offspring the basic genetic message was effectively immortal and could be passed on indefinitely.

For genes to take advantage of any beneficial mutation it was necessary that, having reproduced, the parents die. Parents will not have the beneficial gene (except the one parent in whom the happy mutation has occurred) and by their continued presence would hamper the spread of the beneficial gene and thus jeopardize the survival of all the other genes who are at a survival advantage if they can become a partner to the new star. Thus the genes invented death. Death means that a new gene with a survival advantage of as little as one per cent over the old genes can now spread throughout a population.

You will see that the basic unit of reproduction for a sexual species must now be the gene. At every reproduction there is a shuffling of the genes. The combination of genes in each of the two parents is lost forever. The only things that can be reproduced unchanged are the genes. The whole process is working for the benefit of the genes.

Enough of our aside. The story so far: our replicators have learned to produce proteins and to build cells. They have just learned to build multi-celled organisms. Once this trick had been learned evolution had a field day with it. Soft bodied creatures came first, worms, jellyfish and the like. These were closely followed (closely in evolutionary terms) around 600 million years ago by the first animals with hard parts, shells and bones, for which good fossils remain. Around 300 million years ago fish first learned to breath air and pulled themselves out on to the inhospitable land. These were the first amphibians and their soft, easily dehydrated eggs held them close to the edges of the water.

At this time the plants which had also edged their way out of the oceans on to the land, also clung to the borders of swamps and streams. They too needed water to reproduce, to carry their microscopic swimming sperm.

Then 250 million years ago the first type of wind-carried pollen appeared. Quickly a blanket of green spread over the land. Some amphibians developed into reptiles who laid hard eggs that could withstand a dry atmosphere and they followed the plants across the face of the land. Some of their descendants quickly ballooned into the mighty dinosaurs who ruled the world for the next 150 million years.

Another line developed into the mammals. They had to eke out an existence in the shadow of the mighty reptiles. Among these were the early primates and they have been called the 'rat of the Palaeocene'. But changes were afoot that were to propel this 'rat' from the shadows to the trees and then out of the trees to build in their place the great cities, homes of the 'rat race', that we see around us today.

The world of the dinosaurs was a green monotonous place. Then about 100 million years ago, towards the end of the dinosaurs' reign 'an abominable mystery', as Charles Darwin called it, took place. In just a few million years flowers exploded across the land of the planet. They produced a new and abundant food supply, fruit. Perhaps the dinosaurs couldn't respond quickly enough to the changes that this produced for very soon they were no more.

The primitive primate, the 'rat of the Palaeocene' had been no more likely to evolve into the first 'technological creature', human kind, than any of the other mammals scurrying through the undergrowth in the shadow of the great reptiles. It was the fact that the primates took to life in the trees, to tap the new food available from the sudden emergence of fruits, that was to change all that.

So that we can understand how life in the trees allowed the emergence of human kind we have to make a brief digression. We have to understand just a little more about how evolution works. Evolution can only work by selecting the best available mutations in existing organisms. It doesn't necessarily produce the best possible solution. Think about birds. Superbly adapted to flight, but on the ground reduced to hopping around awkwardly on two legs. Wouldn't they have been better off with a pair of wings and four legs (something akin to a scaled down version of Pegasus the flying horse)?

Probably, but birds developed from four-limbed reptiles. Perhaps they were tree dwellers taken to leaping from tree to tree. Perhaps some of them, through mutation, developed a slight webbing between forelimb and body which, as the limbs were extended in a jump, caught the air. This carried them just that little bit further than others of their species. Perhaps every now and then this allowed them to escape a tree-dwelling predator when others failed. It conferred a slight survival advantage, a slight increase in fitness. So in the next generation there were more offspring with this slight webbing. A further increase in the size of the webbing would be similarly selected for and you can imagine this process very slowly leading to a fully winged creature where the two forelimbs have evolved into two wings.

What you can't imagine is one of these tree-dwelling lizards suddenly beginning to sprout wings leaving the four limbs intact. (This is how many people think evolution is supposed to occur and quite reasonably they have problems with it.) Evolution can only work on what has evolved thus far and this rules out many potentially superb adaptations – like a four-legged bird.

Birds were able to evolve wings because they had forelimbs for evolution to work on and because these could be modified gradually *with each modification conferring a slight additional advantage.*

Now birds didn't evolve forelimbs in order to allow the later evolution of wings. Evolution is quite blind. It has no idea where it is 'going'. The forelimbs developed because they were adaptive in their own right. However, *in retrospect,* we can observe that the presence of forelimbs allowed the evolution of wings. (And the presence of fins incidentally allowed the evolution of forelimbs.) Such 'raw material' for evolution to work on in producing another adaptation we call a *pre-adaptation* and we are now going to explore the pre-adaptations which allowed the evolution of these intelligent, tool-bearing creatures: humans.

TO THE TREES!

So it was that their move to the trees endowed the primates with a set of pre-adaptations which were to make possible the birth of human kind. Each pre- adaptation evolved because it was beneficial to a tree-dwelling life and each just happened to provide the raw material that evolution was to use in producing the first technological creature.

The grasping hand developed to allow locomotion through the branches but was to prove the pre-adaptation for the tool- and weapon-bearing human hand.

A good brain equipped with keen stereoscopic vision and a sense of three-dimensional geometry developed to allow rapid and agile movement through the complex three-dimensional world of the trees but was to prove the pre-adaptation for the still more sophisticated brain and intellectual powers of human kind.

Communication by sound and vision developed, as it did for the tree-dwelling birds, because communication by smell, so favoured by many other mammals, would have proved ineffective in the trees but was to prove the pre-adaptation for human language and writing.

A way of life whereby few young were produced and then carefully and individually nurtured over a long period of time was developed to take account of the roaming tree life and the dangers from predators. This was to prove the pre-adaptation for the long human childhood when the details of our technology can be passed on to the next generation.

This lengthy rearing of the young required the support of a society. A mother giving constant one-to-one attention to her offspring would be at an impossible survival disadvantage otherwise. The need for mutual defence and co-operation in finding scarce but concentrated food sources, such as trees in fruit, would also have required the development of social behaviour. This was to prove the pre- adaptation for the complex social interdependence of the human species.

RETURN TO THE GROUND

All of the primates might have stayed up there in the trees had further changes not swept the lands. About 20 million years ago many forest areas turned to plains and in the cradle of the human race, Africa, our ancestors were forced out of the trees. Initially they were not well adapted to this way of life. This was a new environment and new environments always produce great evolutionary change. Many badly adapted forest dwellers must have tried to 'make it' on the plains. Only those that could quickly adapt to establish themselves were to survive. And so it was, for example, that horses and fast-moving ungulates came about.

Our ancestors took a different course. They began to walk on their two back legs, it has been proposed that this left their hands free for picking seeds and gathering food. Times must have been hard and it is probably at this stage that they had to start killing their first small animals – lizards and birds perhaps – to eke out a living in this harsh new environment. Bigger game eluded them – their tree life had equipped them with no claws or sharp teeth.

Then around 2 million years ago, some people claim earlier, the big breakthrough occurred. These small, ground dwelling man-apes, no bigger than a modern day primary school child, learned to use bones and stones as tools and weapons.

Technology was born.

Now, they could go in chase of the big game. But even with their new weapons they could not do this alone. Hunting required the development of more sophisticated cooperative behaviour, including food sharing. This is still an important social cementer – witness the prevalence of the business lunch as a means to strengthen relationships. This required still greater intelligence and cunning. Hunting would have been difficult for females and their dependent young and so a division of labour with stable social groups and pair bonds was required. Still more sophisticated communication and language had to be developed to coordinate the hunt. Even our lack of hair and numerous sweat glands are attributed to the need for body cooling in the chase of the hunt.

It is easy to comprehend why some have called hunting the 'master activity' for the human race. For it is this activity above all others that has made us what we are today. Indeed there is a popular conception born of books by the likes of Desmond Morris that we are still essentially hunter apes replete with the evolutionary baggage of our past but with business, sports and even war as the 'surrogate hunt'. There is value in this view but, as we shall see, the full picture is more subtle and far more fascinating.

The first tool using man-ape (by tradition the use of tools qualifies the use of 'man') still had a relatively small brain and there now took place an explosive increase in the size of the human brain.

There's an old biological law that the development of an individual traces the evolution of the species. We see a sudden increase in brain size of the human foetus just before birth and it seems that we are witnessing a replay of this mysterious explosive evolution.

Exactly why this took place is unknown – sudden increases in the size of an organ are always hard to fathom – because they happen so quickly they leave a poor fossil record for us to study. However, it is almost certainly significant that this took place soon after man learned to use tools. Probably the ability to use tools that little bit more intelligently conferred such a huge survival advantage that greater brain size and intelligence was rapidly selected for. Perhaps this involved warring between neighbouring tribes – a bit like an evolutionary 'arms race' with brain size the arsenal being built up. Just as in the business world today we are familiar with 'galloping technology' with each new innovation fuelling the need for still further innovations, so human evolution entered an upward spiral of 'galloping brain growth'.

Human kind was a success and so we moved out of the cradle of humanity, Africa, and to lands further North. Here an important part of survival was protection against the weather and, no doubt born of this need and during an ice age about 450,000 years ago, the second big technological breakthrough came: fire.

Fire must have been a huge asset to early humans. In addition to providing warmth it warded off predators and allowed them to cook meats. However it took another 400,000 years, until just 50,000 years ago, for the next technological leap to be discovered using fire: the smelting of ores to make metal. Even at this stage this technology was only wielded by small, roaming hunter–gatherer bands – their roaming lifestyle ruled out larger groupings.

Then, some 10,000 years ago, came the next large technological leap: the invention of agriculture. The times between the technological leaps so far have, in human terms, been vast. Even so the time between them is diminishing rapidly. You may well have already noticed the seeds of exponential growth. Agriculture gave rise to fixed settlements and evidently freed more time for creative thought as the pace of technological advance continued to increase.

About a thousand years ago it had accelerated so that each century was producing a handful of important inventions or discoveries. Then, around AD 1400 in Europe, the critical threshold was reached and technology went into super-exponential growth. The fifteenth century gave rise to 200 important inventions or discoveries and by the nineteenth century this had grown to over 2000. The final count for the twentieth century will be astronomical.

With technology growing so quickly, you could be forgiven for not talking of human evolution over recent millennia but concentrating on technological evolution (as I have just done in this whirlwind résumé of our development). Nevertheless, the evolutionary pressures on human kind during this time must have been huge and substantial evolutionary changes can occur in just 100 generations given satisfactory selection pressures (we know this from theoretical models and from experiments on other species).

Just imagine some of the forces for selection at work during this period. Imagine the early agricultural settlers expanding across the lands of the remaining hunter–gatherers. It must have been something akin to a primitive 'cowboys and indians' with, no doubt, the primitive hunter–gatherers faring no better at the hands of the early settlers than did the (hunter–gatherer) indians at the hands of the (agricultural settler) cowboys. The 'cowboy' genes then and now burgeoned while the 'indian' genes all but vanished.

Think of the impact of birth control. For most of our history we made no connection between sex and babies (there are a few primitive tribes today who still don't). Sex was for fun and babies 'just came'. All that was required for survival was a desire for sex and a desire to look after babies *once they arrived* (hormonal changes during pregnancy see to this). Now women can decide whether they want babies before they experience the hormonal changes of pregnancy. Any genes which dispose against wanting babies are at a 100 per cent evolutionary disadvantage. There can hardly ever have been such enormous selection pressures at work. I would suggest that in a hundred generations there will be a universal overwhelming urge to have babies among the human race.

So not only does our evolution have a great deal to do with the way that we behave with our technology and our businesses (the main thesis of this book), but our technology is having a profound and ongoing effect on this evolution.

Despite the fact that we must be evolving fast even now, evolution is a slow process when compared to the rate at which the modern technological world has exploded on the scene. We are, to a very large degree, pro-grammed by our genes for fitness-maximizing in a different world. Many of our characteristics today evolved when humans were small bands of hunter–gatherers roaming the African savannahs. They evolved when we had sticks and bones at our disposal as weapons and not nuclear weapons; they evolved when we lived in small bands and tribes and not huge cities; they evolved when our main threats were dangerous predators not hostile takeover bids; they evolved when people co-operated to hunt in small bands not to do business in vast industrial enterprises. You will not be sur-prised to learn that in many ways they are outmoded and even dangerous.

GENES – THE GREAT DELEGATORS

You may now ask how it is that human kind seems to survive quite com-fortably in the space age with a set of instincts grounded in the 'evolution-ary wisdom' of the African savannah or before? Genes do not influence human behaviour by prescribing exactly how we should behave. As we saw, human instincts can be overridden by, for example, militaristic indus-trial management techniques. Why is this?

We have to ponder how genes exert their influence. As we have seen, apart from making copies of themselves, all they can do is build proteins. Through this mechanism they direct the building of a 'body' to carry them and during this slow process they can equip their body with instincts: instructions from the genes dictating how the body should behave in given circumstances. They can't have any influence after this stage – the influence of genes changes only during reproduction with the shuffling and trading of genes during sexual reproduction or with the occasional mutations.

Think of the genes as the chief executive officer of a company, with the rest of the company representing the body. Some CEOs are autocratic and insist on making all the decisions themselves. This is particularly prevalent in small companies where the small size and lack of complexity allows them to behave in this way. So it is with some simple organisms – they are slaves to the instructions of their genes. An amoeba – a single-celled organism – cannot learn from experience: it relies solely on the instincts programmed in by its genes.

In larger more complex organizations it becomes more and more difficult for the CEOs to cling to their autocratic ways; in order to solicit the speed of response that the company requires to survive they must delegate day-to-day decisions to the rest of the organization. So it is with more complex organisms. The genes have built brains which can learn from experience and adapt behaviour on a day-to-day basis.

Of course there is a continuum. The presence of a brain doesn't signify full delegation to it by the genes. Take the stickleback fish for example. It has some ability to learn and profit by experience but its genes keep it securely on a tight reign. It has for example an instinctive urge to attack other male stickleback, which it recognizes by their red chests. So rigorously do the stickleback genes enforce this rigid rule that one researcher even reported that his male fish would threaten the red mail trucks as they passed outside.

Human genes are much better delegators; in fact they are the supreme delegators – after all they have the most 'complex organization' to run.

But our genes have not abdicated their managerial responsibilities. Like a good CEO they determine strategic directions and goals. The people on the ground may be making the day-to-day decisions but the CEO is constantly at hand reminding them of the corporate goal; a goal founded in the evolutionary wisdom of the past.

Though we experience nothing as unsubtle as the stickleback's urge to attack the mail truck, we are constantly reminded of our 'strategic direction' by our genes: they tell us what to enjoy, what to dislike. Richard Alexander (1979), a sociobiologist, summed it up like this:

> happiness . . . is eating and sex and parenthood and warmth and touching and ownership and giving and receiving and loving and being loved; it is the cessation of pain and the onset of pleasure; it is finding a way to win; it is having a magnificent idea or a grandchild. . . Happiness is a means to reproduction.

Freud said that the human mind aims to reduce tension and if tension is the result of fitness-reducing circumstances this too amounts to the same thing.

The adolescent human with no mate in a western society chooses to frequent discos and bars populated by available members of the opposite sex, to listen endlessly to pop music focusing almost exclusively on pair bonding (falling in love), to buy the clothes that will gain acceptability with young members of the opposite sex, and so on. All relatively complex conscious decisions but the strategic direction that the genes have set is abundantly clear.

The study of behaviour as explained by genes and evolution is a surprisingly recent phenomenon. It gained its name, 'sociobiology', in 1975 from the great Edward O.Wilson. You may be surprised that it has taken so long to start systematically applying evolution to the study of behaviour. Palaeontologists have been digging up fossils and tracing the evolution of anatomy for centuries. But explaining behaviour by evolution is not so easy – behaviour leaves few fossils. Thankfully, as we shall see, the pioneer sociobiologists are piecing together the evolutionary basis of our behaviour by an ingenious array of techniques.

The teachings of sociobiology has far-reaching implications for anyone requiring an understanding of the human animal (sociobiology necessarily has more to tell us about the individual than the wider group, business or society) – and this should apply to none more than the business person. A philosopher once remarked that the truth about man is inside him. It appears that this is so, and it is perhaps time that we in the business community started looking there.

IN SUMMARY

WHAT HAVE WE LEARNT?

Our biology affects our behaviour in a multitude of profound and subtle ways. The force that is responsible for this is evolution.

That evolution started thousands of millions of years ago when, by some fluke, a molecule arose that could make copies of itself. As it made copies, there were errors. Some of the errors were useful and the molecules that contained the error became more successful, while the original versions died out. Evolution had begun. Once started, the process gradually produced ever more complex life: the first cells, multi-celled creatures, fish, amphibians, reptiles. Some of the reptiles became dinosaurs, others became mammals, who cowered in the shadows. The world of the dinosaurs was a dreary green place, then flowers exploded across the earth and the first fruits arrived. Perhaps it was all too much for the dinosaurs. Soon they were gone and our ancestors took to the trees. They became the primates. The world became a drier place 20 million years ago. Our forest homes were decimated. We took to the ground as small-time hunter–gatherers. Then 2 million years ago came the first tools and we could start to hunt big game. Half a million years ago came fire. Fifty thousand years ago we learnt to smelt metal. Just ten thousand years ago we developed agriculture. Technology was starting to 'gallop'. During the fifteenth century there were 200 notable inventions, by the nineteenth 2000. The total for our century will be incalculable.

But we have come too far. Evolution is much slower than technological change. We are still equipped with the evolutionary wisdom of the hunter–gatherer on the African savannah.

We survive in the modern world because, unlike many less complicated creatures, *our* genes equip us with a set of *inclinations*, not a set of rigid instructions. Just as the CEO of a hugely complex business has to set a direction and then delegate to the rest of the organization, so our genes give us these inclinations but also a mind that can learn from experience *and even learn to over-ride some of these inclinations.*

It is as well that we do learn this. Many of our inclinations are hopelessly inappropriate for today. They lead people to perform below their potential, think poorly, learn poorly, become demotivated and deceive. If we understand how, we can actually take action to prevent these.

We also have some fantastically useful inclinations. They can lead people to co-operate, innovate, communicate and inspire. If we understand how, we can take positive action to harness these capabilities.

WHAT CAN WE DO ABOUT IT?

Put your understanding of evolution to use. Read on!

3

YOUR MIND
and how to get the most out
of it

❖

There is reputedly a sign hanging in IBM's Tokyo office which reads: 'IBM: FAST, ACCURATE, STUPID. MAN: SLOW, SLOVENLY, SMART.' The fact that the world's foremost experts in computers (if not in business management given their recent track record) need to remind themselves that there are vast differences between a computer and a human demonstrates the propensity that business people have for thinking of people in simple mechanistic terms. This attitude has been fostered by industrialization. Mass production reduced many people to 'bio components' of a larger industrial 'machine'. We all appear to have become too used to this sad and unnatural state of affairs. Now technology is (mercifully and at last) relieving people from the drudgery of mass production lines and number crunching. But we tend to feel that, because computers can do the work of such unfortunates, somehow this demonstrates an essential similarity between people and computers or even the superiority of computers. Hence IBM's need to remind themselves that this just isn't true.

If there is a common ground between people and computers it is more in the hardware rather than in the software department. This may seem strange: computers are silicon, metal and plastic and we are flesh and blood. But there is an essential similarity: in a human brain, as in a computer, everything is ultimately written in binary code – everything is ultimately written in a code of 1s and 0s.

The *tangible* differences are in the software. Computer programmes have been produced to perform every type of task from mundane word processing and spreadsheet packages to sophisticated expert systems. Each programme has a different objective. For the word processing package it's typing letters and reports; for an expert system it may be advising financial advisers on the most appropriate investment strategy for specific clients. Ultimately, however, the human brain (or indeed any animal's brain) contains just one huge programme for answering the question, 'What is the best thing for me to do to maximize my fitness (to survive and pass on as many copies of my genes to the next generation as possible)?'

To help answer this question, the brain is pre-programmed from birth with the evolutionary wisdom that its species has acquired over the millennia. In this chapter we will learn that much of the programming that the human brain has amassed is awesome and how many of its tricks are beyond our current comprehension. However, once again we will also see that much of our evolutionary 'wisdom', accumulated by the primitive, hunter–gatherer humans on the African savannah is woefully out of date in the 'space age'. An understanding of some of the strengths and the weaknesses that evolution has equipped our minds with can be a great asset to you as a business person.

DATA VERSUS INFORMATION

Perhaps the first thing to understand about the human brain is that long ago in its evolution it had to learn a distinction that many business people find hard to comprehend today. That is the difference between data and information. Data, according to my dictionary, is a series of observations, measurements or facts. Information on the other hand is the *results* derived from the processing of data according to programmed instructions. Raw data has a tendency to be pretty useless. An oft quoted illustration of data, as opposed to information, is a telephone directory that isn't in alphabetical order. Most companies are awash with data. Information (such as your alphabetized telephone directory), on the other hand, can be useful. The more useful the information, the better the programme that processed the data into information. This ought to hold true by definition. The elegance of the technical means by which data is converted to information should be irrelevant. But as business people, we are all too often distracted and confused by such issues. Executive Information Systems supposedly allow executives to dip into data bases holding all a company's data and pull out and analyse relevant parts. Surely the senior executives who commission these ought, above all others, to be able to define and insist they obtain the information that they require. Apparently not. It is now estimated that around 70 per cent of such systems are failures.

Evolution is a far more ruthless judge of whether a programme is effective or not. If an animal's brain is well programmed, it tends to survive and if not, it tends to die. Evolution has taught animals' brains the difference between data and information and between good information and bad information. Modern computer programmers don't have quite the same incentive to appreciate the difference between data and information. Perfecting their programmes isn't usually a matter of life and death for them. But for their companies it can be – particularly in the case of powerful modern computers which can process enormous volumes of data at the speed of light. The programmes can submerge their organizations in data and still the computer happily crunches out more.

Our hardware, our brains, are far less impressive when it comes to speed. Unlike electricity, which travels at the speed of light, nerves are painfully slow. As an illustration, and appropriately enough, the nerves that carry pain are among the slowest. Have you ever, for example, put your hand on something hot, sensed that you have touched something and then slightly, but perceptively later, felt the pain? This happens because nerves carry signals by means of a self perpetuating electro-chemical reaction. A chemical reaction causes a change in electric potential and this triggers a further chemical reaction further down the nerve which in turn causes a further change in electrical potential. It's slow. But it can be speeded up by insulating lengths of the nerve fibre with fatty cells.

The insulation stops the chemical reaction from occurring, but the electrical potential reaches over to the next naked bit of nerve fibre and its chemical reaction fires off. Instead of slowly passing up the whole nerve fibre, the nerve impulse jumps from gap to gap between each of the insulating fatty cells. Of course all these fatty cells take up precious space in the body, so this is not a trick afforded by every nerve cell. Only those nerves in which it is *vital* to carry information fast are coated in this way. Nerves carrying touch are so honoured, so that, as we run and dart around our world, our brains receive the fastest possible feedback. These fast, fatty coated nerves run from your skin, into your spinal cord and up into your brain. The fatty coated nerves are grouped together and, if you slice across a spinal cord you can see the 'white matter' (white because of the fat).

The speed of transmission for pain cells evidently was not so critical in our evolutionary past. They aren't bestowed with the fatty cells, so pain impulses travel more slowly. Looking again at the spinal cord you can see 'grey matter' where these slower fibres run. And that's why you feel the touch before you feel the pain. (Actually evolution has to some extent mitigated the disadvantage of having slow pain fibres. Pain can trigger off a reflex withdrawal of your hand from the source of the pain before the pain impulses even get to your brain. A simple reflex loop in the spine allows the pain impulse to trigger the nerves that cause you to pull away your hand.)

But what's the point of this interesting (I hope) aside? Well you will be used to referring to your brain as 'grey matter'. And the description is technically correct. The part of the brain that does your thinking is 'grey matter'. It doesn't contain the fatty cells to speed up the nerve impulses. If it did you'd need a head the size of a house to hold your brain. So, the processing speed of your brain is slow – infinitely slower than that of the PC sitting on your desk.

However, evolution has developed some solutions to the problems posed by the tardy 'processing speed' of human brain cells. The first of these is known as 'parallel processing'. This simply means that your brain can co-ordinate many different activities at the same time; it can simultaneously regulate your heartbeat, breathing, temperature, balance and a myriad of other things. But even this capacity is not enough. There is a huge and constant avalanche of data descending upon your brain. It is produced by all the nerves entering the brain. These carry data (not yet information) from all your bodily functions and senses.

Think how overwhelming this could be. Just imagine if you were constantly responding to everything in your field of vision as you read this book, you'd never be able to concentrate on reading. Then there are all the smells, the sounds, the temperature of the room. There seems no end to it. If we tried to analyse and deal with all of it, we'd fast become the ultimate case of analysis paralysis. We simply wouldn't get anything done.

To avoid this situation, our consciousness evolved. What, you may ask, is your conscious mind? The conscious mind is the part of the mind that works on a very select set of **information**, about the world around us now and in the past (memories) to decide what actions we are actually going to take. It doesn't receive raw data, it receives highly processed information. The information that our conscious minds receive is data processed by programmes written by aeons of evolution. Epicharmus pointed out two and a half millennia ago: 'Only mind has sight and hearing; all things else are deaf and blind.'

There is never any prospect of ever being entirely 'objective' about the world. We never receive the raw data that we would need. As Pascal said, 'The heart has its reasons that reason knows not.'

It's all rather like looking at the accounts in a company's annual report and hoping to visualize accurately what's happening to the company. You get some idea, but the financial data has been so processed (with all the profit smoothing and so forth) that a true view is impossible. Nevertheless, as you browse through the notes to the accounts (tucked away on cheap paper and in small print in the hope that you won't read them), you learn more and more about the way that the raw financial data was processed and this gives you a view of the company which is closer and closer to reality.

In this spirit, we are now going to review some of the pre-programmed software that you were born with and think about why it evolved and what it means for your day-to-day business life.

SHORT CUTS

Our brains have learned from their evolutionary past that, given their abysmally slow processing speeds, it is not effective to search through the whole of our memory every time we need to make a decision. It just wouldn't be practical. It would take far too long. (This is, in fact, one of the fundamental ways in which the human brain differs from a computer.)

Somehow the brain manages to compare the situation in hand with other sequences of information that approximate in some way to it. These other sequences can be inherited, inborn assumptions about what the world is like and the best way to behave in certain circumstances or they can be past experiences that approximate to the current one. By running through these sequences, perhaps not in an entirely 'logical' fashion, the human brain somehow produces its remarkable insights, ideas and of course mistakes.

It is the fact that the current situation calls up memories and associations which have a hazy and seemingly illogical link that is one of the human mind's greatest assets. It allows us flashes of insight that are denied to any machine. It is why Elbert Green said: 'One machine can do the work of fifty ordinary men. No machine can do the work of one extraordinary man.'

We can all recall examples of such leaps of insight in our business lives. Just over a decade ago, Smith Kline and French, a lacklustre medium-sized pharmaceutical company, developed 'Tagamet', the first effective treatment for duodenal ulcers. Nobody expected monumental profits from this new drug – after all, the current market for anti-ulcer drugs (which was mainly antacids) was so small. Conventional wisdom held that you had to price not too far above the existing, cheap drugs for treating ulcers. If you'd pro- grammed a computer with the conventional wisdom and given it free reign, no doubt this is what would have happened. Fortunately Smith Kline and French relied on a human. At its primary launch in the UK the pricing deci- sion was pushed to the Financial Director, as this was not such an important drug. Unimpeded by conventional wisdom, he was free to think as only humans can. The existing therapies don't work and the alternative is expen- sive surgery, he reasoned. Tagamet was competing with surgery, not antacids. He set the price accordingly. Soon Tagamet was the best selling pharmaceutical of all time.

So, the brain's ability to produce amazing insights results from its taking short cuts – short cuts that it is impelled to take because of its painfully slow processing speed. However, for every such flash of insight that these short cuts produce, they also produce many errors. If we understand how and when these errors arise, we can take action to prevent them. This in turn will render us much more capable of benefiting from our flashes of insight.

As we have seen, our brains have to make some memories more avail- able to our conscious minds than others. The trouble is that what is made available is determined by our evolutionary past as hunter–gatherer apes and not as aspiring rational managers. This leads to all sorts of errors of judgement. A whole area of psychology is, not surprisingly, devoted to these errors. Judging by the first thought that comes into your mind is called (by psychologists) the 'availability error'. There is a huge catalogue of experiments that demonstrate such errors.

Here is one such simple example (Higgins *el al.*, 1977). The subjects of this experiment had to learn a list of words. They were split into two groups: one learnt terms of praise – 'adventurous', 'independent' and so forth; one learnt terms of reproof: 'reckless', 'stubborn' and the like. Then, as a supposedly separate exercise, they read a story about a young man, his hobbies, his friends, his feelings about himself. They were then asked to evaluate the man's character. Those subjects who had learned the unfavourable adjectives thought much more lowly of the young man in the story than did the group who had learnt the favourable adjectives.

This is simply because their recent exposure to the unfavourable adjectives meant such terms were at the forefront of their minds – they were *available.*

This is a reasonable short cut for evolution to equip our minds with. Recent events are more likely to be representative of the situation facing us. On average, it might be best to search our data bases – our memories – for such events.

Evidence from the vast number of experiments investigating 'availability error' suggests that, alongside recent events, there are specific types of event that tend to be 'available'. Particularly highly emotional and dramatic, image-laden events.

It seems entirely reasonable that these *should* be highly available. Emotions are stirred by events that profoundly influence our fitness (love – prospect of a mate; fear – prospect of personal injury and so on). Experiences associated with emotional events are therefore likely to be very important and relevant. Similar logic would apply to dramatic events.

Most of our evolution occurred at a time when we hadn't evolved speech. (As we shall see later, perhaps surprisingly, most of our communication remains non-verbal to this day). Again, it seems quite reasonable that powerful images should be readily recalled.

But all that was during our evolutionary past. Today in a sophisticated business environment, it is, more often than not, the wrong events that become readily available when we are trying to make decisions. For example, one manifestation of the availability error is the so-called 'halo effect'. The halo effect occurs when our perception of one aspect of something colours our perception of all other aspects. For instance, you may be reviewing a job application with untidy handwriting. Your negative view of the quality of the handwriting will probably colour your judgement of everything else to do with that application.

You may not believe that you would be so small minded, but there is experimental evidence to back this up. When identical examination scripts were reproduced in good and bad handwriting, the poorly written scripts consistently received considerably lower marks.

The availability error, therefore, is one of the key reasons that people's intuitive judgement in making complex decisions is always suspect, in business or anywhere else. (As one wag has put it – intuition is that sense that tells you you are right, whether you are or not.)

An alternative to – and in some senses the complete opposite of – intuitive judgement is actuarial judgement. This involves a rigorous, statistical review of the validity and weight of possible predictors based on past experience.

There have been over 100 studies comparing actuarial and intuitive prediction. In the vast majority, actuarial prediction was better. What's more, intuitive prediction has not fared better *in a single study.* Many of these studies have been related to the world of management and business such as personnel selection, predictors of job satisfaction and future growth of corporate share prices.

I once worked for a pharmaceutical company that was doing rather well. It had a number of big-selling products. These products enjoyed good sales because they contained safe and effective drugs. But pharmaceutical products on the whole don't just contain drugs. They also contain excipients. Excipients are inert sustances like sugar or starch or gum that are mixed with the drug to turn it into a medicine that you can take. And one of our excipients turned out not to be inert. It wasn't harming patients, but it was harming the environment and soon the excipient in question was facing impending global bans on its production and use.

Unfortunately, the products that contained this excipient generated most of our sales. We would have to reformulate all of them if they were to remain on the market. This was not going to be easy. These were complex products. Developing an entirely novel formulation and proving that it was safe and effective in humans would be a risky and very costly undertaking.

We had many threatened products and limited resources. Some of these products were big sellers and some were relatively unimportant. Most of our management wanted development products to replace every product. The prospect of losing sales from any one of them is a dramatic and therefore highly 'available' thought.

The strategists in the company undertook a laborious and 'rational' analysis of how we should deal with this problem. They concluded that we would do better to adopt a 'belt and braces' approach for our big sellers with a second development programme in case the first failed – even if this meant not developing replacements for our smaller-selling products. This made sense because the extra 20 per cent probability of being able to replace a £100 million product that a back-up development programme affords is more valuable than a 50 per cent chance of being able to replace a £10 million product.

The strategists were right, but they couldn't persuade anyone of the logic. The power of the imagery associated with not replacing the £10 million products was too overwhelming – too 'available'.

Fortunately, we had a wise MD. Not only did he possess the intellect to see the logic of the strategists' analysis, he also had the people skills to communicate the situation (where they had failed). The big products were the key to the company's survival he explained. They represented a 'cliff-edge'. If they went down, we were doomed. We had to protect them at all costs. We had to have a back-up development project for each of them, even if this meant sacrificing smaller products.

These replacement projects even became known as the 'cliff-edge projects'.

This taught me a valuable lesson. It is necessary and right to avoid intuitive decision making, particularly in complex situations. But you are then going to have to communicate and sell those decisions to people who will judge them intuitively. *Decide logically; communicate dramatically.*

So far, in considering the 'availability error', we have looked at how to *avoid* 'innocent' errors. It is also, unfortunately, possible to manipulate, or be manipulated, through this phenomenon.

Allow me to demonstrate. Contemplate this simple but elegant little experiment. One group of subjects was asked to estimate, quickly:

$$8 \times 7 \times 6 \times 5 \times 4 \times 3 \times 2 \times 1$$

On average, they estimated the answer to be 2250. A second group were then asked to estimate.

$$1 \times 2 \times 3 \times 4 \times 5 \times 6 \times 7 \times 8$$

On average, they estimated just 512.

So, we have enormous differences in estimates for the *same calculation* caused by a variation in the order that the numbers are presented in.

The phenomenon that explains this is known as the 'anchoring effect'. People are unduly influenced by what they see first when assessing a situation. It is a variant of the availability error. Unscrupulous market researchers can make great capital out of such effects.

One variant of the 'anchoring effect' is that people tend to vary little from the centre of the 'rating scales' so often used in market research. For example, if you ask people how satisfied they are with your new product on the following scale:

very dissatisfied, dissatisfied, satisfied, very satisfied

you will encourage people to respond with a fairer answer than if you asked using the following scale:

dissatisfied, satisfied, very satisfied, extremely satisfied

because respondents will anchor on, and therefore respond near to, the middle of the scale.

Another undesirable manifestation of the anchoring effect occurs when people are assessing the likelihood of the time required to complete a large scale project.

Usually a large scale project – like the design of a new car or the development of a new drug – comprises a great number of activities. The chances of each of these individual activities going wrong or being delayed can be very small. And people anchor on these small possibilities. What they fail to appreciate is that the cumulative probability of failure or delay (when you combine all those small probabilities) is usually very high indeed. I have worked in companies who consistently make huge underestimates of the time it will take to complete *every single project* they undertake.

Still another mutation of the availability error is the 'representative error'. This occurs when people wrongly assume that if something looks more typical or representative, it is more likely to occur. For example, if you throw a die six times, which is most likely to occur, a sequence of:

$$3, 7, 5, 1, 7, 2$$

or of:

$$6, 6, 6, 6, 6, 6$$

Most people would conclude that the upper sequence is more likely as it appears random whereas the coincidence of six sixes in a row is far more unlikely.

Of course, both sequences are equally likely (or unlikely). There is a one in six chance of the die landing on any given number each time it is thrown, irrespective of what has come before. Therefore, the probability of a die landing in *any* given six figure sequence is $6 \times 6 \times 6 \times 6 \times 6 \times 6$ to one.

Why people think the first sequence is more likely is because it looks a more typical sequence. It is, to them, more representative of the sequence you are likely to arrive at if you throw a die six times. It is not difficult to imagine some of the problems that this sort of error can lead managers to make.

Another example from my own experience serves to illustrate this. The pharmaceutical business has, with some fairness, been described as 'molecular roulette'. Drug research and development is a highly risky business. Companies have a 'pipeline' of drugs in R&D, some of which they hope will succeed to reach the market to defray the huge costs involved in drug development.

I have been involved in many strategic planning exercises where future revenues from the products in development are projected. Companies as a rule, will not envisage the possibility where all the products fail and none make it to the market. They will always insist on building in sales from at least one or two. I am convinced that this is a manifestation of the 'representative error': if you develop a large number of drugs, most will drop out of development, but a few will be developed and marketed. That is why the industry as a whole survives and prospers. This is managers' view of what is 'representative' for our industry.

All but the largest companies, have just a few products in development. The chances are heavily stacked against each of them. It is highly likely that none of them will make it to the market. But, this is not 'representative' and so it is a scenario that is not considered and is not planned for.

It may be worth reminding ourselves at this point of Poincaré's famous remark: 'Mathematics is the language in which we cannot express nebulous or imprecise thoughts.' As we have seen, our intuitive thoughts tend to be just that, nebulous and imprecise. That is why it is always a good idea to write down and quantify decisions. Otherwise our minds will decide on the basis of what is 'available' and what is available is determined by a largely irrelevant evolutionary past.

MODEL BUILDERS

Another short cut that our brains take because of their very limited processing speed is to build 'models' of the important parts of our world. When a piece of information relates to one of these 'models' it allows a rapid assessment of appropriate responses and allows that new piece of information to be stored for efficient future retrieval as a part of that model. Just as importantly, information that doesn't fit with one of these models can be regarded as 'noise' and ignored.

There is a strange and wonderful experiment that has demonstrated just how people concoct 'models' of reality (cited in S. Sutherland *Irrationality – The Enemy Within*). Subjects were told about two firemen; one was an exceptionally good fireman, the other was not. Half of the subjects were told that the 'star' fireman was a genuine risk taker. The other half weren't.

Now, here's the strange part: the subjects were later told that the firemen didn't in fact exist. Nevertheless, when they were asked to suggest what might make someone a successful fireman, the subjects who had been told about the (imaginary) successful and risk-taking fireman, still felt that risk-taking was an important key to success. The other subjects, who hadn't heard this bit of fantasy, didn't.

This is an elegant little demonstration of how people build a 'model' to explain things and that that model has a life of its own – it persists even after the information that was used to construct it has been removed.

However, our propensity to build models can, in today's setting go much too far for our own good. Bertrand Russell has said: 'Man is a credulous animal and must believe something. In the absence of good grounds for belief, he will be satisfied with bad ones'. This may go a long way in explaining why managers spend so much money on unproven methods for helping them predict an unpredictable future.

Take personnel selection. Any rational review of the various techniques to assist in the selection of future brilliant performers has to conclude that none of them have been shown to work reliably. Nevertheless, around 85 per cent of the largest continental European companies employ graphologists in personnel selection. This despite the fact that authoritative reviews consistently agree that the validity of this technique is virtually zero. Our instinctive need for some sort of framework, some sort of model on which to base our decisions, seems to override this.

We don't exclusively demonstrate a need for models when it comes to predicting the future; we crave them when it comes to explaining the past. In the area of corporate success and failure, people seem to need some explanation as to why successful firms succeed and unsuccessful firms fail. They are all too often quite satisfied with superficial explanations based on vague but plausible notions. *The Economist*, for example, mused in June 1992 that

> much of the sociological research into corporate behaviour...looks suspiciously circular. Even number crunching analysts are likely to look for things to praise, like care of customers and employees, about the managers of highly successful firms and things to condemn, like selfishness, about the managers of corporate dogs.

Advertisers and marketeers are especially interested in the models people build in their minds. Stephen Leacock in *The Garden of Folly* described advertising as the 'art of arresting human intelligence long enough to make money from it.' In fact the opposite is true. Making money out of advertising requires an acute understanding of and ability to manipulate, not suspend, human intelligence.

The seminal work in this respect is undoubtedly *Positioning – The Battle for Your Mind* by Al Ries and Jack Trout (1981). The secret of success for Ries and Trout is, if possible, to be the first product in an area so that it is your product that is firmly built into the customer's 'model' of this 'portion' of his or her world. To quote Ries and Trout (1981):

> What's the name of the first person to walk on the moon?...the second? What's the highest mountain in the world?.... the second?...The first person, the first mountain, the first company to occupy the position in the mind is going to be awfully hard to dislodge.
>
> 'Kodak in photography, Kleenex in tissues, Xerox in plain paper copiers, Hertz in rent-a-car, Coca in cola, General in electric.

Why is being first into the mind so important and so valuable? Because, once a 'model' is constructed it is very robust and resistant to change. (We saw this earlier with the firemen.) If these models weren't robust, they wouldn't help overcome the brain's limited processing speed. Constantly questioning the models' validity would use up the processing time they are there to save! So if your product is the first to become bound to the relevant model in your customer's mind, it is likely to stay there.

This in large part explains the huge value of brands to companies. It is not the products themselves that are valuable; it is the fact that the brand names and identities form a part of the models that have been built by millions of customers.

Of course this means that if you can't be first, any attempt at a head-on assault against the brand that *is* first is, in all probability, doomed. Again and again the marketplace deals out a severe dose of hubris to companies who are arrogant enough to think they can go head-on against an established market leader.

RCA's attempt to diversify into computers in the early 1970s testifies to this point.

> 'RCA fires a broadside at No. 1,' said *Business Week*.

> 'RCA goes head to head with IBM,' said *Fortune*.

> 'We've invested far more to develop a strong position in the computer industry than we've ever put into any other business venture,' said a confident Robert W. Sarnoff, chairman and president of RCA. 'By the end of 1970, we'll be in a strong No. 2 position.'
>
> Unfortunately, there were some robust models out there in the minds of his would-be customers. And IBM was firmly ensconced in them. The result was depressingly predictable: 'The $250 million disaster that hit RCA,' screamed a headline story in *Business Week* towards the end of 1971.

But, while this sort of challenge is usually doomed, there are approaches that an appreciation of how the mind works can lead you to.

What you have to do is find another of the mind's 'models' where a competitor product isn't already established. Or, as Ries and Trout put it, '*cherchez le créneau*': 'find the gap'. This requires lateral thinking and courage. Quoting Ries and Trout again:

If everyone else is going east, see if you can find a *créneau* by going west.
A strategy that worked for Christopher Columbus can also work for you . .
. For years, Detroit auto makers were on a longer, lower kick . . . Enter the
Volkswagen Beetle. Short, fat and ugly.

The whole point of this is that there is a linkage in the customer's mind –
a 'model' – between certain cars and the virtues of 'bigness' (power, status,
comfort and so forth). This is already established and is robust. However,
there isn't yet a linkage between cars and the virtues of 'smallness' (economy, fun and so forth) There is an opportunity to establish a new model
which will then be robust and highly resistant to change. That's exactly
what VW were able to do, to great commercial gain.

If you can't find a vacant 'model' (or '*créneau*'), you may, as a last resort,
have to attack the established leader. A head-on assault, as we have seen, is
probably doomed. But, there is hope. The models in a mind are not simple,
discrete entities as I have been implying. They are hazy and overlap and
intermix with each other. The perception of an established competitor's
product will be hooked into a number of 'models'. The secret is to ignore
the 'positive' one that is responsible for the product's success and find and
reinforce less positive associations.

The classic example is the story of Listerine mouthwash. When Procter
and Gamble took on the leading US mouthwash, Listerine, with their own
'Scope' product, Listerine's position seemed unassailable: Listerine was a
strong mouthwash. It worked and everyone knew it – 'the taste you hate,
twice a day' proclaimed its ads.

If they had adopted a 'head-on' approach, P&G might have concocted an
even stronger formula and an even bigger advertising spend. They would
probably have failed. But, P&G looked for the weakness in Listerine's
strength. And Listerine's strength was its strength. 'Medicine Breath' is how
the P&G ads described the loyal Listerine users and up shot the sales of
Scope. P&G had detected and played on an established perception or
'model' relating to the unpleasantness of clinical, medical smells. They had
also shown a rare appreciation for the way people think.

HABITS

Still another way that the brain has bypassed the limited processing capacity
of the conscious mind is through habits. A habit means that if a task is performed repeatedly, its execution gets delegated to the unconscious mind
and it is performed 'automatically'. This frees the conscious mind for other
matters. You can see that it's a good idea. You can, for example, listen to
the radio while you're driving your car, because much of the driving is performed by habit, without being conscious of it.

But habits can also be very dangerous. Let's look at the realm of the operations manager. Habits can mean that more frequently performed tasks tend to be done in error in place of less frequent ones. Broadbent (1987), an eminent industrial psychologist, has described it thus:

> Because familiar actions are released unintentionally . . . there can be spectacular and embarrassing disasters when an experienced person does something that is quite unintentional . . . a train driver may cancel a warning signal, as he is used to doing when passing early warning signals; but *this* time he should have taken the necessary steps to slow down. Less drastically, many of us will have had the experience of starting to drive forward at a traffic light when the neighbouring lane moves; until we notice that they are filtering down a side turning and our lane is still stationary.

Habits also release the conscious mind for day dreaming. Researchers have shown that 'stimulus independent thought' (which is what they call day dreaming) can also block the uptake of information from the senses. This can lead to horrific accidents that a computer would never allow. Many terrible plane crashes have been caused by pilots being so familiar with the normal routines that they carry out certain actions by habit. This sets them off day dreaming and this prevents them seeing or hearing the danger signals that would normally provoke them to take steps to prevent the crash.

Habits can form, not just for mechanical tasks like flying a plane, but for our whole approach to doing business. Often, in fast-moving situations, habits can be useful. If, for example, you are a bond trader, you need to make split-second decisions to realize profit opportunities before they disappear. A collection of habits can be a great asset. As Publicus Syrus said in the first century BC, 'While we stop to think, we often miss our opportunity.'

But, habits can also be debilitating for a corporation. The same habits may afflict a whole organization. Perhaps this is largely what a corporate culture comprises. And once established habits are hard to break.

Strong corporate cultures seem to be viewed these days as universally desirable. But, in a fast-changing environment, a collection of habits has as much chance of being inappropriate as appropriate, and once they have been established it can be almost impossible to shift them.

As Cor van der Klugt, an ex-president of the ailing electronics group, Philips, said in 1988 of his struggle to overhaul the corporate culture of the sprawling conglomerate: 'You have a lot of well drilled regiments and all of a sudden you say you want commandos. You can give them a different cap and uniform and they don't know what to do.'

In their book *Corporate Culture and Performance* (1992), Professors John Kotter and James Heskett, both of Harvard Business School, found that strong-cultured firms seemed almost as likely to perform poorly as their weak-cultured rivals. They concluded that the widely held belief that a strong culture leads to strong business performance is 'just plain wrong'.

Corporate cultures can take decades to evolve, the professors believe. The best way to expedite the process, they say, is to appoint an unconventional outsider, like Jack Welch of GEC or Lord King of British Airways.

Shaking off habits *can* be well worth while. Breaking out of habitual ways of performing in an industry has provided some of the most startling success stories.

The Economist noted in May 1993 that some of the most startlingly successful companies of the past decade, such as Wal-Mart and Del Computer, have deliberately abandoned the traditional way of doing things in their industry and, with the help of computer technology, pushed through innovations which have dethroned market leaders. Wal-Mart computerized its stock control system allowing greater customer choice and knocking Sears off the top spot in the process. Del became one of the world's largest computer companies by using computer technology to sell direct to customers, thus doing away with expensive dealer networks.

Habits are also the biggest threat that our evolution has bequeathed us within today's dynamic setting. Many of the gravest threats to the world economy today can be seen as the results of habitual decision taking.

In the early 1970s the Arabs quadrupled the price of oil. Soon they had a mountain of cash that needed a home. Western banks took the money and lent it at double digit interest rates to the governments of Latin America. These countries promptly acquired treble digit inflation rates and went bust. With hindsight it is clear that the corrupt, dictatorial regimes in Latin America should not have been expected to invest the money wisely. There was no evident prospect of their being able to service the massive debt that the western banks were foisting upon them. So why on earth did they do it? It seems that it was simply out of habit. Government loans had always proved safe before. The banks did not see the exceptional nature of these loans (they were gargantuan). They simply failed to perform their 'due diligence' out of habit.

There is a memorable passage in John Burke's (1989) book *The Management of Luck* where he describes the sinister habits of the board of a pharmaceutical company that he once sat on:

> Apparently someone had pointed out that [one of our product's] microbiological count [the number of bugs in it] was too high. What were we to do? Quick as a flash, the Technical Director had his answer: a variety of radiations would lower the count. What would it cost? The Financial Director threw in the figure. Marketing Implications? The answer was ready. Zap, zap, zap around the table. The scene ran like a Hollywood movie – punchy chief executive has his people in place, rips from one to the next, and in minutes carves out the solution. 'OK,' he said at length, 'we'll do it.'

Here we see a classic example of how a combination of perspective-narrowing stress (caused by this domineering chief executive) and a habitual way of approaching work leads to constricted, lacklustre decision making. Fortunately, on this occasion John Burke interrupted this habitual approach to problem solving: 'Who says the microbiological content is too high?' he asks (it turns out to be a competitor) and 'Which micro-organism?' (the human bowel already has a hundred thousand micro-organisms per square millimetre – if there are already millions of this micro-organism down there, what's the harm?').

Most people don't give up their habits without a fight. After all they are, just like the mental models we build, there to save valuable brain processing time. If they weren't robust, if we gave them up lightly, they wouldn't be the processing-time-savers they are meant to be.

Professor Shoji Shiba, the Japanese business guru, cites three attitudes that are key to our defending entrenched mental habits: The Not Invented Here Syndrome (NIH); the I Already Know It syndrome (IAKI) and the Prove It To Me Syndrome (PITM). When he lectures he pins up three signs: 'NIH', 'IAKI' and 'PITM' – each with a line through it.

CONCENTRATION

Not everything about our pre-programmed software is bad news. We saw earlier in this chapter how the mind can, because of its strange structure, produce astounding leaps of insight. Another great asset that our evolution has bestowed upon us is the ability to concentrate.

Unfortunately, just as we saw that the stresses in business can prevent our flashes of insight, so the business environment can conspire to rob us of our ability to concentrate.

This ability to concentrate is a unique feature of the human brain, as compared to that of the other primates. Again this comes back to the fact that, unlike the other primates, we evolved from tree-dwelling herbivores into land-dwelling carnivores and hunters. A monkey has a huge and dispersed supply of food fruit spread out in the canopy of trees and will flit from tree to tree collecting many different small prizes. The hunter is different. It just needs the one kill to sustain it for a great time. Like the wolf who follows the herd of buffalo for days and weeks waiting for its chance, like the cheetah who stalks the herd of zebra for hours waiting for a single indiscretion by one of the herd, concentration proved to be the key to success for humans, the huntering man-apes.

This required evolution to modify greatly the human brain. It involved the development of the specialized frontal lobes. This is why you have your high forehead as compared to other apes or indeed our distant ancestors. (You are, no doubt, familiar with artists' impressions of 'man-apes' with their low sloping foreheads.) What do our large frontal lobes do? If a monkey sees fruit, it goes and picks it. There is seldom any problem with this. If a hunter sees his prey and adopts the same approach, he will almost certainly fail. He has to bide his time. He has to wait for the propitious moment. He has to take actions, like long stalkings, for which there is no immediate payoff, for which the reward is delayed. He has to have evolved the idea of 'deferred gratification'. This is a key part of what the frontal lobes of our brain do; they maintain a balance between action and restraint.

Sometimes, as a treatment for chronic depression (which is in a way a pathological propensity for inaction), these frontal lobes are surgically disconnected. (You may well have heard of a 'frontal lobotomy'.) It can help the depression, but you can guess the drawbacks: without his or her frontal lobes, a person's ability to 'hold back' is severely constrained. The results can range from undue frankness and indiscretion to outright aggression.

In business, the ability to bide one's time is repeatedly cited as an undeniably important advantage. Lord Weinstock of GEC even went as far as to say that the best business people 'always leave decisions to the last possible moment'.

Another effect of lobotomy is an inability to concentrate over long periods. So if you take a dog, a good concentrator because it's a hunter, and put a piece of meat in one of several boxes, a minute later it'll be able to go straight to the correct box and retrieve the meat. Disconnect its frontal lobes and it's completely confused about which box to go to. Its mind appears to have wandered; its powers of concentration have gone.

The great Peter Drucker didn't pull any punches when he highlighted the importance of concentration in business: 'Concentration is the key to economic results...no other principle of effectiveness is violated as constantly today as the basic principle of concentration . . . Our motto seems to be: "Let's do a little bit of everything." '

Benjamin Disraeli held concentration as being of paramount importance too: 'The secret of success is constancy of purpose.'

So why then is it that modern business people, their foreheads bulging with special frontal lobes, provided specifically to allow them to concentrate, appear to have such difficulty in concentrating? It seems that in the modern business environment it is all too easy to 'unlearn' or override what ought to come naturally. Companies invest huge amounts of money in computers, photocopying machines, periodicals, etc., etc., seemingly so that they can deluge their employees with data. They then spend large amounts of money sending people on time management courses to teach them how to ignore most of it.

In attempting to harness our powers of concentration for business (powers which evolved for hunting), references to hunting are often used in literature. In my view, the pick of the crop when it comes to time management books, *Time Management Made Easy* (1987) by Turla and Hawkins, is a perfect example:

> Elephant Hunting – Set Goals and Bag the Big Game! . . . An important key to being successful with time-management is to make elephant hunting your highest priority. This means to go after your big, high-payoff goals every day and to minimize the time you spend stomping on ants, those trivial details that take up so much time.

Does the importance of harnessing our powers of concentration suggest another reason why 'leaders' are in such demand today? Is it because people who have the ability to set clear goals are so much better at harnessing our innate powers of concentration? The problem today is not a lack of desire to concentrate – that comes naturally to human kind. It is, perhaps, being able to see, in a vastly 'over-communicated' society, *what* we should concentrate on. Berkely Rice said that 'Visionary people are visionary partly because of the very great many things they don't see.'

Many successful companies have summed up their strategic vision in a way that focuses the concentration of the organization; the family motto of the perennially successful shoemakers Clark's is 'But will it sell shoes?'; Komatsu, the Japanese earth-moving equipment manufacturer that took on and humbled Caterpillar where so many had failed, lived by the slogan '*Maru C*' or 'surround Caterpillar' (a vision that allowed it to attack every chink in Caterpillar's armour); Canon lived by the simple creed 'Beat Xerox'; NASA wanted its 'man on the moon' (and look how 'grounded' it's become since it has had no such vision).

Time and time again successful companies have harnessed people's natural ability to concentrate (if only they can see what to concentrate on).

MENTAL OVERLOAD

Concentrating on a goal and performing a range of different tasks to achieve it is one thing. Concentrating effectively on a mundane, repetitive task is quite another. We noted at the outset of this chapter that such tasks are best replaced by technology. This is not only because humans think slowly, but because they often think inaccurately. We have seen that the conscious mind has a limited storage capacity and processing speed. It is ultimately for this reason that the brain, unlike a machine, cannot reproduce mechanistic actions with unfailing accuracy. But there are still jobs that require a high level of mechanistic behaviour of people. An understanding of how the brain works can be a great help to operations managers.

Capacity overload is a frequent cause of errors. Consider machinists: industrial research shows, not surprisingly, that as the number of alternative actions for an operative rise, so does the likelihood of making a mistake.

Problems of capacity overload are exacerbated by the fact that, because the brain does not structure its thoughts in an entirely 'logical' way, it does not rigorously compartmentalize activities. That's why you have problems with tongue twisters. Two slightly different words coming close together are liable to be jumbled.

The same problem can occur in an industrial setting. Similar activities can be confused and jumbled. In the words of Broadbent again:

> One act may incorrectly replace another similar one. Hence if a task involves a set of push buttons, adding a second task that also uses push buttons will be more confusing than a task that also uses sliding levers. On the display side also, adding visual signals for a second task to a visual display will be more confusing than adding an auditory task. Further, given the limits of the internal speech form of temporary memory, an overload could be produced by two tasks that both use internal speech. This could be true even though each task alone would produce no difficulty.

IN CONCLUSION

We have seen in this – and the preceding chapter – that the human mind is capable of amazing insights and creativity, if only we can release it from constraints like stress and habit. Isn't it worrying therefore, that senior executives continue to ignore the importance of thinking? Korn/Ferry's 1990 *Executive Profile: A Survey of Corporate Leaders* represents interviews with 1708 senior executives from the Fortune 500 companies, including commercial banking, life assurance, diversified financial, retailing and transportation companies. The study indicates clearly that executives believe that the single most important factor in bringing about success is hard work. 'Don't work smarter, work harder'.

You can just imagine all those bankers burning the midnight oil to close another mega-loan to the Latin Americans! This fact becomes all the more interesting when you juxtapose it with another: a third of the Fortune 500 industrials listed in 1970 had vanished by 1983.

Perhaps, then, we should close this chapter, as we opened it, with a quotation from IBM. We will close, in fact, with the motto of IBM:

'Think'!

(It's a pity – as we shall see in Chapter 8 – that they didn't!)

IN SUMMARY

WHAT HAVE WE LEARNT?

The human mind is – just like your PC – a binary computer. However, whereas a PC can run a variety of programmes to accomplish various tasks

– from spreadsheets to word processing – the mind contains just one huge programme for answering the question: 'What is the best thing for me to do to maximize my fitness (to survive and pass on as many copies of my genes to the next generation as possible)?' The programming contains the 'evolutionary wisdom' of our hunter–gatherer ancestors. However, it is not necessarily wise to use all of the programming in a modern business setting.

This huge programme has to run on hardware (your brain) which has a pitifully slow processing speed when compared to your PC. Evolution has equipped us with mechanisms for coping with such tardiness, most notably a conscious mind. The brain filters and processes the huge volume of raw data emanating from our senses and from our memories and presents a small, manageable amount of highly select information to our conscious mind to allow us to decide upon a course of action. This entails the taking of a number of pre-programmed short cuts.

When presented with a problem, the brain doesn't run through all its memory (as a computer would). In some poorly understood (and not necessarily 'logical') way, it compares the situation with other memories that approximate to it. This can and does produce amazing flashes of insight.

However, other short cuts can produce sloppy, irrational thought. For reasons which made good 'evolutionary sense' in the past, the brain has a tendency to favour memories of recent, emotional, dramatic and image-laden events when it comes to deciding which to make *available* to the conscious mind. The sort of error in reasoning that this can produce is known as the '*availability error*'. It is a major cause of irrationality and poor decision making in business.

Our minds have a tendency to produce 'models' of aspects of our world and then reject the inconsistent or superfluous. Such is our propensity to build models to explain and simplify our world that it can make us unhealthily credulous and susceptible to fads such as graphology. These models, once created, are robust (if they were constantly questioned they wouldn't save processing time). This explains consumer behaviours such as brand loyalty and tells us much about how to achieve it.

Habits – the automatic, rather than conscious, execution of frequently performed tasks – are another time saver. They can have appalling consequences ranging from catastrophic accidents to pathological corporate cultures with fixed and inflexible ways of doing things.

Our ability to concentrate on a single goal for prolonged periods and to direct all our activities towards it is unique among primates. It stems from our hunting instincts and is the key to business success. The modern business environment, however, seems to be designed to undermine this ability.

But, while the mind can be good at concentrating on a goal, it is bad at performing repetitive tasks accurately. This is because of its limited processing speed and inability to compartmentalize data rigorously.

WHAT CAN WE DO ABOUT IT?

O   Don't look to computers, or textbooks for innovation. You need a wonderfully sloppy human mind (preferably – as we saw in an earlier chapter – one freed from stress).

O   Don't rely on your intuition. Particularly where complex decisions are involved, the availability error will ensure that you make poor decisions. Force yourself to write down and quantify complex decisions.

O   Don't allow your mind's propensity to build 'models' make you overly credulous. Resist techniques like graphology and psychometrics that have not been validated – however comforting it is to believe them.

O   Understand that the models other people build in their minds *are* their reality. They are very robust and if you offer them something that is superfluous or inconsistent, they will reject it. This applies not least to product offerings and marketing. While you can strive to be rational, no one else will!

O   Harness habits in fast-moving situations like bond trading.

O   Smashing corporate cultures takes drastic action – an unconventional outsider as boss seems your best bet.

O   Harness people's powers of concentration by defining clearly what their goals are. Don't leave it to them, or assume it's obvious – the modern business environment conspires to distract people.

O   Replace people with machines for repetitive tasks. If you must use people, design the tasks to prevent mental overload. Avoid exceeding their capacity; make different tasks as dissimilar as possible to avoid confusion.

4

OTHER PEOPLE'S MINDS
and how to get the most out of them

❖

Chapters 2 and 3 have been about thinking. In the first of these we looked at thinking under stress – because stress is such a part of the fabric of business life and because it puts such a damper on creative thinking. In the second the brain was visualized as a thinking tool – because the brain has strengths and weaknesses which we can build on or minimize with the aid of a little understanding.

These chapters were primarily about how the mind reacts: how it reacts to certain circumstances; how it reacts to certain problems. But perhaps of even greater importance to business people is encouraging people to be proactive not reactive. This comes down to two overlapping tasks: how to motivate people to do a good job and how to get them to learn to do a still better job.

Most managers accept that motivation is a *sine qua non*. Whatever else you do, a business cannot be successful without motivated people. As the oft quoted saw has it: 'Organizations makes things possible: people make things happen.'

The fundamental importance of learning is perhaps less widely appreciated. The effects of learning is one of the most powerful forces driving the structure and consolidation of industries. It is largely because of learning that a Ford Escort today costs less than a Model T Ford in real terms.

The concept that explains and quantifies the importance of learning in industry in known as the 'learning curve'. The learning curve was popularized by the Boston Consulting Group who, in 1966, conducted a study for a semiconductor company. They found that the real costs (in other words after adjusting for inflation) of integrated circuits were dropping by 25 per cent for each doubling of cumulative experience (the number of circuits manufactured). These cost savings didn't simply relate to labour productivity; they related to component costs, advertising costs and just about everything else.

Since then many studies in many industries have shown cost declines of 10 to 30 per cent with each doubling of experience. Not one study has failed to show a learning effect.

The Japanese are obsessed with organizational learning. One of the most commonly used words in Japanese business is *Kaizen*. It means continual creeping improvement. We don't have an equivalent word. A popular saying in Japan that captures this urge to carry on finding every possible way to improve things is 'Pursue the last grain of rice in the corner of the lunch box'.

In 1984, Mazda employees submitted nearly three million suggestions for improvement, 70 per cent of which were implemented.

The Japanese obviously know a thing or two about what motivates their employees to come up with and learn new and better ways of doing things. They are intuitively in touch with human nature in this respect. So, let us take a look at this nature.

WHY BIOLOGY FAVOURS AN 'ENLIGHTENED' APPROACH TO MANAGEMENT

Here is an aspect of animal behaviour that managers should constantly bear in mind: all animals have a tendency to remember and repeat what they enjoy and forget and avoid what they dislike.

Why is this? Taking the latter, the things people dislike, first, Professor Norman Dixon (1988) has summed it up as follows:

> some 'dimmings' of memory have in the past had considerable survival value. Without them how could people have 'picked up the pieces' after such appalling setbacks as the Black Death, the Tangshan and Tokyo earthquakes which together killed over a million people, and the crash of Wall Street, immediately after which (but only for a very limited time) people committed suicide in droves. Without them what mother just recovered from the agonies of childbirth would ever risk doing it all again, and what escapee from a hideous marriage would ever contemplate another matrimonial entanglement?

Now let's look at what people enjoy. But what is enjoyment? David Barash (1981) explains it like this:

> Why is sugar sweet? Because it contains sucrose, of course. What is the evolutionary explanation for sugar's sweetness? Clearly, just as beauty is in

the eye of the beholder, sweetness is in the mouth of the taster. To anteaters, ants are sweet; anteaters may even find sugar bitter – certainly they don't like it as we do. The reason is clear enough: we are primates and some of our ancestors spent a great deal of time in trees, where they ate a great deal of fruit. Ripe fruit is more nutritious than unripe fruit, and one thing about ripe fruit is that it contains sugars. It doesn't take much imagination to reconstruct the evolutionary sequence that selected for a strong preference among our distant ancestors for the taste that characterized ripe fruit. Genes that influenced their carriers to eat ripe fruit and reject unripe ultimately made more copies of themselves than did those that were less discriminating.

Not only do certain foods taste sweet, but we find certain behaviours sweet. We enjoy friendship, eating, drinking and making love for exactly the same reasons that we find sugar sweet: doing these things helps increase our fitness. They make it more likely that we will survive and reproduce and pass copies of our genes on to the next generation.

Not only do we find these activities 'sweeter' (we prefer to do them), we also find memories of these activities 'sweeter': memories of enjoyable occurrences are filed in our brains so that they have priority of access to our conscious minds over other memories. The reason is simple enough to understand: by recalling the sweetest experiences, the ones most likely to ensure our maximum fitness, we are likely to repeat the behaviour that brought them about, and to repeat the experiences.

But our evolution has taught us that certain functions are more urgent that others. We have to make sure we can breathe before we start worrying about shelter. Hence we are programmed to give certain needs priority over others. This has long been recognized by social psychologists.

Maslow's Pyramid of needs

The most famous classification of human kind's 'hierarchy of needs', one much quoted in management texts, is that of Maslow, the 'pyramid of needs'.

A person is motivated by the lowest level need, until it is satisfied. Then he or she moves on to the next.

Increasingly today, talented people satisfy the lower three or four levels with relative ease. If you try and motivate your most confident, talented individuals by undermining their safety and security needs (by intimidation and threatening the sack, etc.), they will simply move on to another job.

This goes a long way to explaining why, again and again, research has proved that an 'enlightened' approach to management which focuses on giving people fulfilment in their jobs, recognition, praise, and above all responsibility, tends to result in better productivity and better results.

WHY ARE THERE SO MANY UNENLIGHTENED MANAGERS?

Why then, in the face of all this research, are there so many 'unenlightened' managers, who insist on using fear and coercion as their prime management tools? The answer lies, I believe, in the statistical phenomenon of 'regression to the mean'. Don't be put off; it's simple enough.

Say you're a sales manager teaching a salesperson to produce the latest sales spiel. If you ask her to make a number of presentations they will vary in quality. Most presentations will be reasonably close to the average (the 'mean'), but occasionally there will be exceptionally good or bad presentations. This variation is quite normal. The object of training your salespeople is to improve their average (mean) performance. Some will always be better than others.

Let's say that while you're out in the field with her you witness an absolutely appalling sales presentation. Despite all the evidence that it's the wrong thing to do, your instinct may be to shout and scream at your salesperson. It may be the wrong thing to do, but just look at what happens to her performance. Even if your screaming has done nothing to improve her and indeed even if it has slightly decreased her average ability, it's almost certain that her next presentation will be better. This is because extremes in performance are unlikely and uncommon and, by the laws of chance, it is very likely that the next performance will be closer to the average or mean. The performance will have 'regressed to the mean'.

Assuming that you know nothing about 'regression to the mean', this acts as further proof to you of the power of a good roasting. But let's say you're open minded enough to give a more enlightened approach to management and that you will at least try the effect of praising very good performances (although deep down you're sure it'll be to no avail). The phenomenon of 'regression to the mean' is at work again. Let's say you witness an exceptionally good sales pitch. You're delighted and, as you clutch that valuable order, you festoon your salesperson with praise. And so into the next call. Chance dictates that your woman will produce a performance closer to her average and, even if your praise has raised that average somewhat, her next attempt will not match the one that you just praised so unreservedly. There you are: not only does a good roasting improve her performance, but praising worsens it. QED . . .

'Regression to the mean' is a charter for the unenlightened manager. So, we need to take a somewhat more relaxed and long-term view of the effects of enlightened management.

BIOLOGY PREDICTS NO PANACEAS WHEN IT COMES TO MOTIVATION

Enlightened management is not merely a matter of heaping praise on employees at every opportunity. It involves treating people as the inordinately complex and subtle creatures that they are and not subjecting them to crass management dogma. And dogma unfortunately forms the basis of many managers' understanding of motivation.

Their understanding of learning and motivating is akin to the 'carrot and stick' approach. Although they don't know it, they are subscribing to what is known as 'Classical Learning Theory': people have a very general ability to learn and when an activity is immediately followed by either something pleasurable (a reward) or unpleasurable (a punishment) then that activity is, respectively, more or less likely to be repeated in the future.

On the face of it this makes perfectly good sense. One can easily see how and why such a method of learning would evolve. Pleasurable things are good for fitness, unpleasurable bad. By repeating activities associated with pleasure and avoiding those associated with displeasure we should increase our fitness. Furthermore, if an activity is going to be good or bad for us, it's reasonable to assume that we would be aware of this quickly. This suggests that rewards or punishments must follow quickly to have an effect.

But evolution has produced something more subtle and what follows illustrates the strange ways rewards and punishments can affect animals. It is not a recipe for a workable scheme for running improved sales incentives or the like. The effects of rewards and punishments have not been studied well enough in humans. I therefore cover this ground as part of your 'liberal arts' education as a manager. It will not give you access to any new techniques, but it will make you far more open minded about varying rewards and punishments to find the best combination empirically. It will give you a healthy scepticism of 'simple fixes' and it will reinforce your appreciation that animals and people are complicated and wonderful things. So how does 'Classical Learning Theory', seemingly reasonable at first sight, fall down?

To begin with, different rewards will produce different results according to the circumstances. To understand how and why, consider a rat in a 'T–maze'. A T–maze is simply a walkway with a T–junction at the end so that the rat can turn either right or left. If you put a thirsty rat on the T–maze and always put its reward, water, down the left-hand arm, it will quickly learn to always turn left at the T–junction. If, however, you put a *hungry* rat on the T–maze and always put its reward, food, down the left-hand arm, it takes it much longer to solve the problem.

The reasons relate to the world in which the rat and its ancestors find either food or water. Bodies of water often remain in the same place. Therefore it makes sense for a rat to keep returning to where it has previously found water. Food, however, is seldom found in the same place twice. It's very quickly consumed by other rats or other animals altogether. There has been no survival advantage in evolving an inclination to revisit the location of past morsels (however tasty they may have been – you see the point about pleasure).

If, however, the location of the reward is occasionally changed, the hungry rats do much better than the thirsty rats. For obvious reasons – the thirsty rats keep, wrongly, revisiting the place where they first found water, whereas the hungry rats continue to search more widely and try both arms of the maze. Here we see an example of different rewards reaping better or worse results according to the task in question.

Also, the effect of punishment differs according to the context. For a simple example, let us return to *hungry* rats again. The rats are presented with food pellets of differing size and flavour. The idea is to train the rat not to take certain types of pellet by using different forms of punishment. First of all electric shocks are used as the form of punishment. The electric shocks succeed in training the rats not to take a certain size of pellet, but they fail to teach them not to take a certain flavour of pellet.

This calls for a different form of punishment to be used, X-rays. The X-rays don't give immediate feedback to the rats, rather they make them feel ill (through radiation sickness) an hour or so later. The results are quite the opposite to those achieved with electric shocks: the X-rays succeed in training the rats not to take a certain flavour of pellet, but they fail to teach them not to take a certain size of pellet.

The environment in which rats live and evolved provides an explanation for this behaviour. The size of an object can often be an indicator to whether it is likely to produce immediate physical pain; certain sized insects may, for example, be more likely to sting. The rat is therefore programmed to consider an association between the size of something and whether it experiences pain. Hence an electric shock can be used to dissuade it from eating certain sized pellets. The taste of a substance is much less likely to give a clue to the likelihood of physical pain. Associating the taste of a food with physical pain is not therefore part of a rat's programming. Accordingly, an electric shock cannot be used to dissuade it from eating a certain flavour of pellet.

Conversely, the taste of an object is much more likely to give a clue as to whether it is 'off', putrid and likely to make the animal ill. The rat is therefore programmed to associate the taste of something with whether or not it feels sick some time later. X-ray-induced radiation sickness can therefore be used to dissuade the rat from eating a certain flavour of pellet. The size of an object is unlikely to give any clue to whether it is 'off' or not and consequently the rat is not programmed to make any association between the size of something it ate and whether it is sick some time later. Radiation sickness cannot, therefore, be used to dissuade the rat from eating a certain size of pellet.

It took a long time for this sort of demonstration of the inadequacies of 'Classical Learning Theory' to emerge. As I said earlier, we have made no real progress in determining how and why types of punishment and reward vary in their effectiveness according to circumstances for human kind. All that we can hope is that by understanding that animals do not have a simple, general capacity to learn and do not respond in equal measure to all rewards and punishments in varying circumstances, you will remain open minded and willing to experiment and vary the mix that you use.

As Rosemary Stewart concluded in *The Reality of Management* (1986), 'Our brief survey of the search for panaceas to solve all problems of management labour co-operation shows that there are none'. And this brief review of animal learning should make you very suspicious of anyone who claims otherwise.

TOTAL QUALITY MANAGEMENT AND BIOLOGY

No matter how hard and open-mindedly you search to motivate, you just won't succeed in making people do it 'your way' all of the time. The reason for this lies in our evolutionary past and it has profound implications for what is probably the biggest business fad at the moment, Total Quality Management (TQM).

The goal of TQM is 'zero defects' in all the activities that a business conducts. What does biology tell us about such a goal?

There emerges a fascinating generalization out of all the animal behaviour conditioning experiments that have been performed. (Behaviour conditioning experiments involve trying to solicit certain actions from animals in response to various punishments and/or rewards.) What emerges is this:

it doesn't matter what you do, you will *never* achieve the desired response from an animal 100 per cent of the time. Generally about 95 per cent is the best that you can expect with an animal after continual reinforcement (rewarding correct behaviour or punishing incorrect behaviour).

Why is this? It is because in the real world in which animals (including ourselves) evolved, no matter how good a behaviour appears, there is always the possibility of greater reward somewhere else. Our rat may find food in a certain place every time he looks, but there may be even more somewhere else and it pays to check other possibilities every now and then. (Just as a company with a world beating product is ill advised to spend *all* its resources marketing it – some money and energy must always go to finding tomorrow's products, to new markets, in other words upon speculative ventures for the future.)

Animals have found it fruitful to invest around 5 per cent of their time speculating, investigating whether there are unrealized, unexplored opportunities for them. (It is, perhaps, an interesting coincidence that companies typically spend a similar proportion of their revenues – 5 per cent – on R&D.)

People are the same. If you try and marshal them into doing something a certain way and into always doing it like that, you will fail. They will experiment with new ways. It's in their nature. And your quality programme will fail.

This is just what seems to be happening. An article in *The Economist* (April 1992) stated that: 'there is increasing evidence that the quality programmes of many western companies are failing dismally'. Viewed one way, this is very good news for all those TQM consultants. They could be in business for a long time to come!

But there is a serious side to this. There is another way to achieve quality, not by prescribing exactly how people should work, but by harnessing their instinctive drive to invest a proportion of their time in finding new and better ways to do things.

The crux of the problem seems to be the inability of companies to aim their efforts at the right target – the customer. Instead they become obsessed with controlling the employee with 'statistical process control' techniques and the like.

Evidence is now emerging that by approaching quality as our biology predicts you should, you will be much more successful. A 1992 study by A.T. Kearney showed that firms who had implemented a successful quality programme were twice as likely to have pushed responsibility for quality down to the shopfloor.

A little respect for our biology can pay big dividends!

RISKY BUSINESS

It seems that people never learn to stop taking seemingly pointless risks. Somehow, just as animals seem programmed to invest a certain amount of time speculating, so they seem to be programmed to take a certain level of risk.

Evidence for this comes in the form of what is known as 'risk compensation'. If life becomes less dangerous in some way, there is a tendency for people to compensate by taking more risks in some other way. Take the phenomenon of 'accident migration'. It is a well known fact that if there is an accident black spot on a stretch of road and something is done to make that stretch safer (like straightening the road), then there is a tendency for there to be a corresponding increase in accidents somewhere else along the road. People drive more dangerously on the other parts of the roads to compensate for the loss of risk at the ex-black spot.

A similar phenomenon occurs if you make people's jobs safer. In Britain, the Health and Safety executive spend over 100 million pounds every year enforcing safety regulations. Interestingly as people's livelihoods have generally grown less risky, there has developed a huge leisure industry which in large part allows people to buy back the risks they no longer take at work.

We seem to be programmed to take a certain, minimum level of risk. Just as in business 'the biggest risk is to take no risk' so our biology seems to have learned the same lesson.

While there may be a *minimum* level of risk that people are prepared to function at, the actual level of risk that they accept will depend on the circumstances. The ability to evaluate specific risks seems to be built into every living creature.

As we saw at the outset of Chapter 4, an animal's mind is a dedicated programme for answering the question: 'What is the best thing for me to do to maximize my fitness (to survive and pass on as many copies of my genes to the next generation as possible)?' All animals seem to have an inbuilt ability to assess the costs and benefits of taking given risks. That's why a rat will attack you when its cornered and not otherwise. It's then that it has the most to gain: it might survive intact with the least to lose: it assumes that if it does nothing will probably be killed anyway. When the rat doesn't feel threatened, it wouldn't dream of attacking you.

People, of course, think in just the same way. When we feel comfortable and unthreatened, we are not inclined to take many risks. When you play it safe, accidents are unlikely. But, as Mark Twain said: 'Name the greatest of all inventors. Accident.' Conversely, when you feel threatened, you are (like the cornered rat) more inclined to take risk. In 1984 *Fortune* magazine identified its 'Eight Masters of Innovation' (cited in Davidson's *Offensive*

Marketing). It then interviewed these companies and discovered that the driving forces behind their innovativeness were commitment to new technology and *the threat* of being outpaced by competitors.

This would lead us to expect that large, successful companies might be inclined to take less risk than is prudent, because they feel so comfortable and unthreatened and there seems to be good evidence for this. Adams and Brock (1986) have reviewed numerous studies and have concluded:

> the smallest firms produced around four times as many innovations per R&D dollar as the middle-size firms and 24 times as many as the largest firms. Nor do giant firms display any appetite for undertaking more fundamental and risky research projects. That is, contrary to the image that bigness is conducive to risk taking, there is no statistically significant tendency for corporate behemoths to conduct a disproportionately large share of relatively risky R&D or of the R&D aimed at entirely new products and processes.

Perhaps this is one reason why (as we saw in the last chapter) a third of the Fortune 500 industrials listed in 1970 had vanished by 1983. Their attitude to risk becomes that summed up in a famous New Yorker cartoon, where the company chairman tells his board: 'What we need, gentlemen, is a completely new idea that has been thoroughly tested.' Some companies, of course, recognize this problem. Mark McCormack, the founder of IMG, summed up the paradox that successful firms face:

> Business is a competition, and any high level, sophisticated competition is almost exclusively a head game. The inner game of business, as this could be called, is understanding the Business Paradox: the better you think you are doing, the greater should be your cause for concern; the more self satisfied you are with your accomplishments, your past achievements, your 'right moves', the less you should be.

Many firms do something about it. 3M, for example, is famous for its innovation. 3M encourages risk taking: 'our people know if a new idea doesn't work out...they'll still be respected and have a job.' And John Harvey Jones ran ICI with the philosophy that, 'If we wish to encourage risk taking, we have to be prepared to accept and recognise that people will fail.'

Our need to take a minimum level of risk and our programming to asses risk is also evident in the area of job turnover. Job turnover has frequently been viewed as a somewhat desirable form of 'natural selection' whereby misfits, those who 'can't take the heat' weed themselves out of the organization. This may happen to an extent, but there is evidence that quite a different phenomenon is also occurring. A highly capable incumbent may view a job that he or she can do easily as not providing enough risk and challenge. Furthermore, that person's considerable talent may lead him or her to view a change of jobs as being a risk worth taking. There is strong evidence that this actually occurs.

Nicholson (1987) has observed:

> Latack's study of hospital professionals and managers changing jobs suggests that people actively seek out the stress of desirable moves, and those who make major transitions exhibit superior adaptive capabilities to those making minor moves. This is confirmed by our recent research, which shows that the most radical job changes may induce marginally more anxiety prior to change than less radical moves, but bestow far greater subsequent rewards in terms of satisfaction, discretion and challenge.

We are, then, clearly equipped with an inclination to quantify and, if appropriate, take risks. Which is not to say that we quantify risk 'rationally'. Our view of risk is heavily coloured by our evolutionary past.

During the Gulf War, international air travel, particularly by US business people, dropped off catastrophically because of the perceived risk of terrorism. This despite the fact that any rational analysis would tell us that there was more chance of being killed in a car crash on the way to the airport than of falling prey to a terrorist.

By looking at our biology, it is possible to see at least an explanation for the way we analyse risk.

If you ask people whether they would prefer to *be given* £50 or take a 50:50 chance of *winning* £100, they will tend to choose the £50. If you ask them whether they would prefer to *lose* £50 for sure or take a 50:50 chance of *losing* £100, they will tend to risk the £100.

These bets have the same 'expected value' (the product of payoff and probability). If you could make either of the bets on offer a great many times, you would end up with the same return irrespective of which bet you chose. Nevertheless, we appear to be *risk averse* when it comes to making a gain (we'd rather have a sure £50 than a risky £100) and *risk seeking* when it comes to a loss (we'd rather chance a loss of £100 than definitely lose £50).

The reason lies in our evolutionary past. We evolved as hunter–gatherers eking out an existence, often on the verge of starvation. Under such circumstances a bird in the hand is literally worth two in the bush. With one bird you would have something to eat; you would survive. With no bird you might be dead. Consequently, there is no sense in your risking having no bird for the possibility of catching two birds.

On the other hand, if you are eking out a subsistence living, *any* loss is likely to be fatal. You would be better to risk a severe setback than accept a definite moderate setback.

This is what explains our attitude to risk and money today and is what economists call the 'diminishing marginal utility of money'. Simply put, this means that each additional pound you gain is less valuable than the last. The phenomenon is a direct result of our biology. The first pound you have can mean a meal and the difference between life and death. The millionth pound makes virtually no difference to your survival prospects.

Furthermore the same root in our biology explains why, in the long run, shares always outperform bank accounts as an investment. Shares are more risky. You may do very well with them, but you may make nothing. Because people are *risk averse* when it comes to making a gain, they will only invest in shares if *on average* they offer a better return.

Our fundamental attitude to risk also explains the agency costs often incurred by failing companies. Agency costs are what economists call managers looking after their own interests rather than those of the shareholders. When an ailing company approaches bankruptcy, if there is no sensible chance of a turnaround, the shareholders would prefer management to put the firm into administration so that as much of the value of the firm can be salvaged for the shareholders. The managers, however, might take a different view. Being *risk seeking* as far as losses are concerned, they will have an unhealthy tendency to risk total bankruptcy if there is a small chance of turning the business round (and saving their jobs) rather than putting it into administration. This aspect of our biology then is one reason why the managers of ailing companies often act in such a cavalier and reckless fashion. (Witness Maxwell and Polly Peck in recent years.)

WHAT YOU LEARN AND WHERE YOU LEARN IT

We have seen, in the context of risk taking in business, that our attitude to risk varies according to circumstances because of our evolutionary past. We will now discover how a similar state of affairs exists as far as learning and recall is concerned.

When it comes to learning and recall, it is wrong to think simply in terms of punishment and reward. You can no doubt recall many events for which there was no overt punishment or reward.

What else could influence your ability to recall? Again, it helps to contemplate our evolutionary past. Let's say, while roaming the African savannah, one of your ancestors was confronted by a pack of wild dogs. He tried to shake them off by swimming across a nearby river. It was no good, the dogs were consummate swimmers and by the time he got to the other side they were nearly upon him. As luck would have it, though, he had come ashore near to a large tree and decided, in desperation, to try climbing it. It worked; the dogs were unable to follow him and he survived.

Months later he was again out in the savannah and once again he was confronted with a pack of wild dogs. What are the most useful memories to have access to right now? Obviously, he would like to be able to remember what happened when he was last in this situation, in this state of mind: what worked and what didn't, so that he can ignore the ineffective actions and repeat those that worked. If he has genes in his body which encourage him to do this, he'll probably shoot up the nearest tree and survive to pass those genes on to future generations; the trait will be selected for. If he has other genes that don't encourage this, he may head for the river, never to be seen again, along with his useless genes.

This is why, when you're in a particular situation or mental state, you tend to remember what happened when you were last in that state. It's called 'state dependent recall'.

How this can affect you as a manager is easily envisaged. You have an important presentation to give to your board and, like the industrious person that you are, you take work home to prepare for it. You spend hours preparing and, to be honest, you rather enjoy it, sitting relaxed at home with your favourite music playing.

But then the day of the presentation arrives. Like most people, you are terrified by presentations to the board. You enter the board room in a cold sweat and when the time comes to start your presentation, your mind is a blank. Why? You prepared so well and two days ago you knew it all. The explanation lies, of course, in 'state dependent recall'. You prepared in a calm, relaxed state and you're now in a worried, tense state. Your evolution has programmed you to recall events experienced in the sort of state you're now in. You'll need to relax if you're going to remember all that stuff. Fortunately you manage to calm down a little and you start to remember what you had to say. The more you talk, the calmer you become and the better you do. In the end you acquit yourself rather well.

That night you decide to go out and celebrate your success. It was an important presentation and you're relieved that it went well. So relieved, in fact, that you rather overdo the celebrations, and the following morning you can remember virtually nothing of the night before. As always in such circumstances you are consumed with the fear that you committed some awful gaffe while under the influence. Still it was an important presentation and its successful completion was worthy of celebration. And indeed the following night you are visited by a group of colleagues who persuade you to join them for a second night of revelries. Strangely, as you begin to drink, the conversation comes round to last night's antics and now, with a few drinks inside you, you find that you can begin to remember what happened. Did you really say that?

You're probably by now in no fit state to ask, let alone answer, the question that really interests us here and that is: why can you now remember what happened last night whereas this morning it was a complete blank? The answer, once more, lies in 'state dependent recall': you remember actions performed under the influence of alcohol best when you are again under the influence.

This all seems to give a certain validity to the role playing that is used on so many business courses. Role playing often recreates the stresses of the job and we should, therefore, be that much better equipped to recall what we learnt.

CAN YOU ACTUALLY LEARN HOW TO DO BUSINESS?

However, role playing may be not nearly enough to bridge the gap between theory and practice as far as business is concerned. Being able to do something in theory and being able to remember something in theory seem, in many aspects of life and in business particularly, to be two quite distinct skills. This difference between academic and practical abilities is supported by the fact that ability in IQ tests does not seem to predict success in life in general. As Professor J.Z. Young (1979) has observed:

> . . . there is growing suspicion that many tests do not in fact predict performance of the abilities they are supposed to measure. Thus MacKinnon (1962) showed that in America the level of IQ (Terman Concept Mastery Test) correlates only 0.08 with creative achievement. Hudson (1966) in Britain found that successful scientists, judges, and politicians had not achieved better university degrees than less successful people. Twenty three percent of Cambridge Fellows of the Royal Society got second- or third-class degrees, against 21 per cent of the control group. Forty-three percent of D.Sc.s got 'seconds' or less. This is only a small sample, but 'success' evidently depends on more than ability in examinations. However the study by Terman and Oden (1962) of 1528 children of high IQ showed that they were consistently successful in their careers for 40 years.

In a sense, this is hardly surprising, considering the inability of workers even to agree on what they are trying to measure when they study IQ. Earlier this century British researchers were still trying to identify general abilities while the Americans were trying to separate out a number of 'elemental' qualities which people could possess in varying measures. For example Thurstone in 1930 isolated seven elemental abilities: V(Verbal), N(Number), S(Spatial), M(Memory), R(Reasoning), W(Word fluency) and P(Perceptual speed). These days it's all changed again and the 'hierarchical view' prevails. This holds that there are a number of different levels of ability – higher levels being broader in nature and containing wider general ability. Take your pick! There is little agreement as to what intelligence means even in the broadest sense (before you even start to think about measuring it). Is it innate potential, a capacity for development and achievement, or is it the ability of a functioning mind which has developed for better or for worse?

But we can be far more specific about the difference between academic and practical abilities as far as business is concerned. Industrial psychologists constantly stress the difference between *knowledge* and *skill.*

Broadbent (1987) has captured the distinction with examples from everyday life and the world of business:

> A familiar example is the ability to produce grammatical sentences in your native language. You can do so without being able to give a formal statement of the rules of the grammar; . . . Again in a business game one can

show that somebody takes the correct decisions about raising a selling price, or decreasing the size of a work-force, to achieve certain goals. Yet in the different context of being asked verbal questions about the task, the same person may not do well.

In other words, some situations seem to call up familiar actions without needing the person to formulate a purpose which can be talked about to other people. Experienced managers faced with a pile of paper describing the business game they are about to play, may start 'automatically' to search out the alternative possible decisions they can take, or to think of past situations from real life or previous games that showed one policy to be better than another. Yet they may not be able to put these strategies into words. . . If the person's experience has been appropriate, so that each complex situation calls out the correct action, such intuitive or 'seat of the pants' decisions may have considerable advantages. Correspondingly it is dangerous to assume that one can learn decision making, management of people, or interviewing by acquiring the ability to answer formal questions about these topics.

This has serious implications for the whole notion of learning about business in an academic setting. Professor Shoji Shiba – the Japanese business guru we met in a previous chapter – has views on the failings of western business schools that underscore these differences between knowledge and skill. The schools put theory first and reality second, he asserts. 'Business is reality' says the professor. 'We have to learn from reality.' His remedy is to steer students (and faculty) on to the shopfloor (just as Japanese firms do for their proto-managers).

But business schools are paragons of practicality compared to economists. Wassily Leontif was the winner of the 1973 Nobel Prize for economics. He is an outspoken critic of his profession's 'preoccupation with hypothetical rather than observable reality'. To prove his point, he surveyed four years of articles in the prestigious *American Economic Review*. The result: more than half the articles were abstract mathematical models; a quarter drew on statistics gathered for other purposes. Only one article made direct use of data gathered by the author. Its subject: utility maximizing behaviour in pigeons.

Perhaps this preoccupation with knowledge as opposed to skill explains the abysmal record of forecasting for the 'dismal science'.

But let's not stray from business. It's not just managers who can achieve practical results without 'academic reasons'. Experienced machine operatives can produce productivity improvements that they cannot 'explain'.

We have already seen that human memory seems to be a highly structured set of associations. A set of associations may be linguistic or **non-linguistic**. Who knows, there may be no words for some of the things that successful business people do. Perhaps the most important way to learn about business *is* just to do it.

Finally, we return to our assertion at the opening of this chapter: 'All animals have a tendency to remember and repeat the things that they enjoy and forget and avoid the things they dislike.' People tend to enjoy activities and techniques that 'work', that 'deliver the goods'. However, they may explain why this activity works quite wrongly. Let me demonstrate.

Consider the Eskimos and their igloos as described by David Barash (1981):

> The Eskimo . . . perhaps the most technically ingenious of all non-industrialized peoples . . . invented the igloo, with its super efficient hemispherical shape, its tunnel entrance (imitated by modern mountaineering tents), and its adjustable door of snow blocks, which can be adjusted precisely to allow in precisely the correct amount of cold air that will quickly be warmed by a seal oil lamp and then rise and escape through another adjustable aperture, this one in the ceiling. Yet, after spending many years with the Eskimo, explorer and anthropologist Vilhjalmur Stefansson found that they could not accept any general statements about the theory from which this engineering marvel was derived – not even the notion that hot air rises. According to these people, the behaviour of the world is governed by gods and spirits, not by laws of cause and effect. None the less hot air *does* rise and although the Eskimo may not 'know' this, they certainly behave as though they do.

Now here's the important lesson, I believe, for business people: if you didn't know all about hot air rising, but you did know that the world is not governed by gods and spirits, you might be inclined to believe that the Eskimo are wrong to construct their igloos so. After all the whole theory that underpins the construction is wrong. However, the Eskimo may not be able to explain correctly why what they do works, *but it does.*

Business school academics scoff at the fact that most practising managers assess investment projects by rules of thumb like 'payback times' and 'return on book'. They can demonstrate that the only academically sound way to assess a project is by calculating the 'net present value of its future cash flows, taking into account the time and risk adjusted value of money'. Other 'rules of thumb' (like how to set advertising spend and how to make recruitment decisions) are similarly derided. But most of the managers in question are actually running not wholly unsuccessful businesses (and the academics are not). Could the managers, their actions honed by the reality of the market and the need to produce results, on occasion be acting like the Eskimo? Could their actions work for reasons that they cannot explain?

Experienced and successful business people have often commented on the deficiencies of an academic training for business. Surely this is connected by the fact that in practical professions like business (and being an Eskimo) one cannot necessarily find words, or the right words, to explain why something works.

Getting results is a skill that cannot be learned in the classroom.

Paul Getty

Life at a university, with its intellectual and inconclusive discussions at a postgraduate level is on the whole a bad training for the real world. Only men of very strong character surmount this handicap.

Paul Chambers

you cannot run a company, a division, or a department with a checklist of things to do or by slavish devotion to a theory devised by the most brilliant professor at a business college, because business, like all of life, is much too vital and fluid to be wholly contained by any checklist, formula or theory.

Harold S. Geneen (1989).

IN SUMMARY

WHAT HAVE WE LEARNT?

Motivation and learning are of fundamental importance to business. It is motivated *people* that make things happen while learning allows them to make things happen better. The economic power of organizational learning is phenomenal. It is a force that shapes entire industries. The Japanese are obsessed with it.

Vital to an understanding of motivation and learning is the fact that people tend to remember and repeat things they enjoy ('rewards') and to forget and avoid things they dislike ('punishments'). But people have a hierarchy of needs ranging from physiological needs (food, water and so on) to self-actualization needs (self-improvement and self-esteem). Once a level of need is satisfied, it doesn't provide a means to reward people any more. Talented people, in particular, find it easy to fulfil lower needs. (They can easily be appointed to another well paid job.) Trying to motivate them by focusing on their lower needs – by giving them more money, or threatening their job security – won't work. A more 'enlightened' approach is required.

Despite this, there are still many unenlightened managers. They think they can see evidence with their own eyes that threatening and criticizing works. What they are actually seeing is 'regression to the mean': an *unusually* poor performance will *usually* be followed by a better, more average one. This is because of the laws of chance, not because of any criticism. An enlightened approach is best in the long run.

However, we have a wholly inadequate understanding of which rewards are best under which circumstances as far as human kind is concerned. All that we *can* say is that, based on animal experiments, the truth is likely to be complex and that, based on business experience, there are no simple panaceas.

Even then, no matter how hard you try, you won't persuade people to do things 'your way' 100 per cent of the time. Evolution has programmed us always to invest *some* of our time finding better ways to do things. This means that 'Total Quality' programmes which attempt to control people will fail whereas programmes aimed at harnessing people's instinct to find better ways to serve the customer will succeed.

There is a similar situation with risk. People are programmed to take a certain minimum level. But, above this minimum level, the actual level of risk taken will depend on the circumstances. Specifically, people will take more risk when they feel threatened. This is why successful, 'cosy' companies tend to be unadventurous and ultimately fail. Although some have found ways to buck the trend.

We don't quantify risk rationally. Our feelings about risk are driven by our evolutionary past as hunter–gatherers. For example, this makes us risk averse where a possible gain is concerned: we would rather have £50 for sure than an equal chance of winning either £100 or nothing. This explains various aspects of commerce and economics – for example why 'risky' shares are priced by the market such that they will always perform better in the long term than 'safe' bank deposits.

Just as our attitude to risk depends on circumstances, so does our ability of recall. We remember things best under the same conditions that we learnt them. Perhaps this is why case studies that recreate a business situation are so popular at business schools.

Even this may not be enough to bridge the gap between theory and practice. Most of our evolution occurred before we developed language. There is a bank of evidence that (verbal) *knowledge* does not lead to *skill* and that experienced business people may have skills that they cannot even put into words.

WHAT CAN WE DO ABOUT IT?

○   Make learning a priority for your organization.

○   When trying to motivate intelligent, talented people, focus on their 'higher needs' of esteem and self-fulfilment, not on their lower needs by paying them more or undermining their security.

○   Have faith in your people. Don't be discouraged when you praise them and they perform worse. You are seeing 'regression to the mean'. Keep building them up. Think about the long haul.

○   Be open minded about reward and incentive schemes. We don't know what works best when. But we know it must be complex.

○   Strive for quality by harnessing people's instinct to find better ways to do things. Don't try to 'control' them. You will fail.

○   Don't let people feel too safe and cosy, or they won't take risks. Remember the biggest risk in business is to take no risk.

○   Don't trust your intuition where risk is concerned. Work out the expected value of any transaction.

○   Remember that if people learn things in real life situations, they will tend to remember them in real life.

○   Employ people with proven business *skill* – a proven ability to produce consistent results. Knowledge alone may not be enough.

5

SEX
and what happened to a
man's world

❖

Gender is a tricky subject, fraught with dangers of accidental and deliberate misinterpretation. But no review of our biology and how it affects managers could be complete without a look at the differences between the sexes and their implications.

The idea that our biology influences our behaviour is strongly resisted, with the best of intentions, by people who oppose sexism. These people confuse men and women being equal with their being identical (at least mentally identical; no one would argue that there are not certain physical differences). These are two completely different issues.

Whether men and women are equal is a moral or political question which concerns the worth of individuals of either sex. I hope that no one reading this book will disagree that all humans should be treated as equal in terms of worth and in terms of their rights to opportunities to realize their full potential.

Whether men and women are identical is a question for science and there is, as you will see, no doubt about the answer: men and women are, in some ways, profoundly different, mentally as well as physically.

Nevertheless, because of this confusion between being equal and being identical, there are people who continue to insist that all differences between the sexes are due to girls being encouraged to play with Barbie Dolls while boys are encouraged to play with Action Men. Barbie Dolls and Action Men may well pander to and even exacerbate differences between the sexes, but to suggest that they alone cause the differences denies all the facts. Indeed, for evolution to have given men and women radically different physical appearances and capabilities and then equipped them with exactly the same mind to control these would be, to put it mildly, a crucial 'design fault' – one that would have put the human race at such a serious survival disadvantage that we would certainly not be here to discuss the subject.

Notwithstanding the above, I will take some time to discuss some of the evidence that the sexes are intrinsically *inclined* to behave in different ways. (Note inclined. There is no suggestion whatsoever that either sex is bound to or should behave in any particular way.) We will then discuss the reasons for these differences and some of the many implications.

First, the fascinating account that follows provides a demonstration that these intrinsic differences between the sexes actually exist.

A rare genetic disease was recently discovered in the Dominican Republic. It causes babies who are in fact male to be born with female-looking genitals. The parents happily start to raise their 'little girl', no doubt encouraging her to play with the Dominican Republic equivalent of a Barbie Doll. However, upon reaching adolescence, when male hormones are released, these individuals revert to typical male behaviour patterns. This occurs in the face of and despite all the conditioning and social pressures for female behaviour. Clearly biology is very much involved in creating 'male' and 'female' behaviour patterns.

Let us now direct our thoughts as to why.

THE GENERAL PATTERN FOR DIFFERENCES BETWEEN THE SEXES IN OTHER ANIMALS

A good starting point is the general pattern of the differences between the sexes in *other animals*. This allows us to be more objective than if we just started talking about ourselves and it allows us to look at animal behaviour less affected by the norms and customs of a human society.

Fitness, as we have seen, is a gene's ability to promote copies of itself in the next generation. Everything that a gene does (or rather encourages the body in which it sits to do) is an investment in the future, in its fitness.

As every business person and investor knows there are two approaches to investment: a low risk approach, where one can be very certain of a modest return (for example a bank deposit) or a high risk approach, where one is very uncertain about a high return (for example venture capital).

So it is with genes: by and large these two opposing investment strategies have been adopted by the two sexes. Female animals have generally taken the 'bank deposit' approach to maximize their fitness: they produce relatively few offspring and they ensure that they have a good chance of surviving to the next generation by concentrating their efforts on nurturing and caring for them.

Male animals, on the other hand, have generally taken the 'venture capital' approach. They produce vast quantities of cheap 'sperm cells'. They can, theoretically, use this to fertilize a vast number of females. Once he has mated with one female, a male animal doesn't have to hang around concentrating all his efforts on raising his offspring; the female, by virtue of her 'bank deposit' approach, will do this for him. A male animal can, whenever the opportunity presents itself, divert his efforts to securing further mates who will bear and nurture his offspring.

The payoff is potentially huge. But, just as in business, the higher the return you seek from your investment, the greater the risk you have to be willing to take. The problem that our typical male animal faces is that all the other males of his species are in the same position: each has the prospect of a bumper genetic 'payoff' if only he can be the one who mates with several females. *In order to stand a chance of securing an 'unfair share' of females and propel a great number of his genes into the next generation, the male has to adopt an aggressive and risky approach to life.*

The elephant seal may to many people epitomize boorish male behaviour. The strongest, dominant male elephant seal establishes a harem of females with whom he mates. Many (in fact most) males, therefore, fail to mate at all. What is the best strategy for male seals to adopt under these circumstances? Obviously he has to opt for a 'reproduction or bust' approach; he will have to fight hard and take risks to become one of the lucky few who pass on their genes to the next generation.

And this is exactly what happens. Right from an early age male elephant seal pups are taking risks in order to grow to be the biggest, strongest bulls. In particular male pups will engage in 'milk thievery'. That is to say they will steal extra milk from nursing seals who are not their mothers. It sounds cute but it can be deadly: each seal mother is making a massive investment in producing milk and she intends it for her own offspring – she may injure or even kill a pilfering pup. But for a male pup, it's worth the risk to steal a lead on the competition.

Meanwhile, female pups suckle contentedly, solely from their own mothers. Their chances of reproduction are relatively high: there is bound to be a high quality, dominant male only too willing to mate with her. It is not worth her while to take the sort of risks associated with milk thievery.

Elephant seals typify the pattern in mammals (and humans are mammals) with the male seeking a high genetic payoff through adopting an aggressive, high risk approach to life and the female seeking a modest payoff through a low risk, less aggressive approach.

DO HUMANS FIT THE GENERAL PATTERN?

This general pattern for animals may appear irrelevant to a modern twentieth century business person. After all, humans seem to adopt an altogether different strategy: men and women pair on a one-to-one basis, and, generally, bring up their one family together. It appears on the face of it that men and women are adopting the same 'reproductive strategy' and so shouldn't their natures be very similar?

But before we can draw any such conclusion we have to be sure that human monogamy (one man paired permanently to one woman) is 'biological' and not just a social phenomenon which overrides our biology.

Whenever a human institution or activity is surrounded with elaborate ritual and public affirmations it's fairly certain that, to some extent, it goes against our biology. Otherwise why go to such elaborate lengths to get people to do what they'd be doing naturally?

In this context, when you think of elaborate marriage ceremonies, it should be warning bells and not wedding bells that are sounding. In fact, in keeping with most other mammals and nearly all primates, humans are, as we shall see, not biologically inclined to total monogamy. To some this may be self-evident – the huge man-orientated sex industry (from girlie magazines to prostitution) does not suggest that males in particular are entirely satisfied with the monogamy imposed by marriage. If the evidence in front of your eyes doesn't satisfy you there is plenty of 'science'.

Animals whose males mate (if they can) with more than one female are known as *polygynous* animals. It is a feature of polygynous animals that males tend to be larger and more aggressive than females. It's easy to think why: larger more aggressive males tend to be more successful in securing females. This is not without its costs. Maintaining larger bodies (with more muscle and less food reserves in the form of fat) makes these males less likely to survive in severe cold and more susceptible to death by infection. It is all part of the risk a polygynous male animal needs to take in order to increase his chances in fierce male–male competition for the valuable females. Polygynous males live a more expensive, risky life. (The venture capitalist comparison, based on my experience of them, continues to hold!)

As you might expect, the more polygynous the species (the larger the successful male's harem tends to be), the larger this difference in size between male and female will be. For example, among the primates the highly polygynous male gorilla is vastly larger than the female.

In monogamous species, as you would expect, males and females tend to be the same size; it is possible for practically all the males to reproduce so there's no pressure for larger males. Again, among the primates, the monogamous male gibbon is the same size as a female.

Let us now turn our attention to humans. Men are significantly larger than women – 5 to 12 per cent larger in fact. This difference is, for example, **greater** than that between the *polygynous* male and female chimpanzee. (So far we humans seem to fit the pattern for a polygynous species quite nicely.)

Another feature of polygynous species is that males tend to reach sexual maturity later than females. This is because in these species there is strong, violent and potentially dangerous competition among males for females. Sexually mature males invite hostility from competitive males. It therefore pays males to delay their maturity until they have the size and experience to stand a chance in the competition for females. Human males reach sexual maturity significantly later than females. (Again we fit the expected pattern for a polygynous species.)

This is merely some of the evidence. There is no doubt: human monogamy is an invention, and a fairly recent one at that. In fact, prior to the Judaeo–Christian ideology, which is largely responsible for the spread of monogamy, over 80 per cent of human societies were polygynous.

Let me stress that by demonstrating that human males are biologically *inclined* to be polygynous, I am not advocating this or providing an excuse for infidelity. We now live in a totally different world to the one in which our biology evolved. Much of our biology is dangerously out of date (a recurrent theme in this book) and this is just one example. There is no doubt that in the 'information age' modern children need a stable home environment in which to grow and learn. Modern marriage is an excellent way of providing this and promiscuity may jeopardize a marriage. The important point is not that we can expect or excuse male promiscuity, but that the two human sexes can be expected to differ in temperament, in certain inclinations, in a similar way to most other polygynous animals.

AN IMPORTANT ASIDE

Throughout this chapter, and indeed this book, we are studying biological inclinations. The genes that determine these inclinations have been selected over the millennia, often in very different circumstances to those that now face us. The fact that something is 'instinctive' or 'natural' doesn't make it good.

If you are in any doubt about this, think of moths. You will have noticed that moths frequently fly into artificial lights. Often they are burnt to death as a result. One theory as to why moths do this has it that, in the past, sources of bright light were invariably celestial bodies (the moon or stars) and moths evolved an ability to navigate by these bright lights. Today bright lights are often artificial lights and moths' tendency to try and navigate by any bright light often results in self-incineration. Would anyone argue that if moths had the mental capacity to understand and control this tendency to self-incinerate, it would not be a good idea to stop it?

In this chapter we will see again and again that the tendency for human males to adopt a more risky and aggressive stance in life is often as appropriate as a moth flying into a candle. Human males in business are no exception.

WHAT DOES ALL THIS TELL US ABOUT THE WAY PEOPLE BEHAVE?

So, let us now consider what predictions can we make from our understanding of the differences between male and female biology? We can see what evidence there is for these predictions and what implications they have for us as business people.

1 RISK TAKING

As we have seen, males tend to adopt a 'venture capital' approach in life: high risk for high gain. Our first and most fundamental prediction from this will be that men tend to live generally 'riskier' lives than women.

You will remember that in our animal example, male elephant seals started taking greater risks almost from birth with their 'milk thievery'. The same appears to be true of humans. There is evidence that baby boys are more 'colicky', they cry more than baby girls. Effectively baby boys are demanding more attention and food from their parents. This is not without its risks: witness baby bashing. But if you want to be one of the biggest, strongest males you need all the nutrition you can get as a baby.

And human males continue to take greater risks throughout their lives. One of the best ways of demonstrating this is to consider the ultimate consequence of leading a riskier life: you are more likely to die. Sure enough, analysis of death rates shows that, at all ages, a greater proportion of men die than do women. In fact men have higher death rates than women for every single form of traumatic and violent death, from drug abuse to sports injuries. Flamboyant, accident-prone behaviour in general (not just fatal forms) tends to be male. Just one example: in the USA 93 per cent of convicted drunk drivers are male.

Despite the evidence that men and women are different, some might still argue that these higher male death and accident rates are because a male upbringing encourages a more risky, accident-prone life style. All the evidence suggests otherwise. For example, in early twentieth-century Kansas, it was common practice to castrate mentally retarded men. It was therefore possible to compare the death rates of castrated and intact men in the same environment (a mental institution). Sure enough the intact men, with male hormone coursing around their bodies, survived, on average, to just 56; whereas the castrated individuals lasted, on average, to the grand old age of 69. (Incidentally, for the same reason, if you castrate your male cat, he too will live longer.)

Hence, we can expect males to be disposed to riskier behaviour in business. This is borne out by the insurance industry, which is, of course, already well aware of this. Males pay higher life premiums than women because their riskier life styles make them more susceptible to premature death. We might expect that unmarried males, who have generally yet to enjoy any reproductive success, would be the most disposed to risky behaviour. Indeed motor insurance premiums reflect just this: unmarried males under the age of 25 have the highest premiums.

It's difficult to quantify the relative risks taken by men and women in business. Usually men and women work in large organizations and it is difficult to isolate the riskiness of any individual's approach to work. But not impossible.

There is one profession that we can look at – fund management – and what follows is my own 'back-of-an-envelope' study into the risks taken by male and female fund managers. 'Investment Trusts' are public companies, but each Investment Trust's assets consist of a portfolio of shares in other companies. This portfolio is managed by a fund manager (or sometimes a team of fund managers). It is possible to measure the riskiness of this portfolio relative to the shares market as a whole. If a portfolio is as risky as the shares market as a whole, then the portfolio is said to have a 'beta' of one. This means that, on average, when the market goes up one per cent, the portfolio goes up one per cent and, when the market goes down one per cent, the portfolio goes down one per cent. If the portfolio is twice as risky as the shares market as a whole, then it is said to have a 'beta' of two. This means that, on average, when the market goes up one per cent, the portfolio goes up two per cent and when the market goes down one per cent, the portfolio goes down two per cent. The higher the portfolio's risk, the higher the 'beta'.

The 'beta' of an investment trust is largely determined by the 'beta' of the portfolio of shares that constitutes its assets. On average, not surprisingly, investment trusts have a 'beta' of almost exactly one. That is to say that, on average, an investment trust is as risky as the shares market as a whole. There are only nine investment trusts with female fund managers in the UK. If you take the average of their 'betas' it is only 0.76. This is a very, very low 'beta'. We can't read too much into this. Nine is a very small sample and in any case females may be given less risky sorts of portfolio. But, just perhaps, biology is creeping into these female fund managers' investment decisions.

Another way to see if maleness and risk taking go hand in hand is to look not at individuals, but entire company cultures. Although groups of people are made up of both males and females, it is possible to estimate the 'masculinity' of various cultures and then to see if there is a correlation between male culture and risk taking.

Geert Hofstede (1980) conducted an interesting (and much more rigorous) study that throws some light on masculinity and risk taking. Hofstede was actually looking at international cultural differences, with a view to seeing how applicable US management theories were in other countries. To do this he chose a highly standardized multinational and suggested that as the company culture was so homogeneous, the only differences between people's attitudes would be due to their national origin. He classified cultures according to four measures and two of these interest us here.

The first of these two measures is how masculine the culture was. Hofstede seems to have had an uncanny insight into biology. He classified a masculine culture as having attitudes that are very consistent with our discussion so far. For example, he cites the following as masculine attitudes: 'Men should be assertive. Women should be nurturing.' 'Money and things are important.' 'Ostentatious manliness ("machismo") is appreciated.' And so on.

The second measure of interest to us is how much risk tended to be taken in the culture. (Actually Hofstede measured the converse of risk taking, 'uncertainty avoidance', but I have 'translated' here for clarity.)

Anglo-Saxon countries (the UK, Ireland, USA, Canada, New Zealand and Australia) all scored above average in terms of the masculinity of the culture and above average on the tendency to take risk. These countries seem in these respects to be behaving very 'biologically': masculinity and risk taking go together.

However, there are examples of a few countries that do not fit this pattern. Interestingly, Germany and Japan, both of whom, like the Anglo-Saxon countries, have a masculine bias to their culture, have managed to combine this with a much lower predisposition towards risk. Viewed in the light of Germany's and Japan's strong economic performance, this becomes all the more interesting. The suggestion that an inability to curb some of the excesses of 'natural' male behaviour may be economically counterproductive is just beginning to emerge.

We could hazard a guess at how these excesses are damaging to business in Anglo-Saxon countries. If you study corporate finance there is a constant need to take into account what are called 'agency costs'. These, as you may recall from Chapter 4, are the costs associated with managers taking decisions and risks that are in their interests rather than the shareholders' interests. For example, cash rich companies consistently take over companies in unrelated businesses. It is well known that the vast majority of these takeovers are unsuccessful and the vast majority of them are later divested.

But the desire to run a huge company seems often to be so great that the management cannot bear to do the best for the shareholders and simply give the excess cash back to them. Haspeslagh and Jamison sum it up by paraphrasing Churchill: 'Shareholders are the most important constituency in an acquisition, except [for] all the others.' Many a destructive takeover battle has raged for this reason. In Japan these hostile takeovers just don't occur. The Japanese have, as a society, recognized their futility. They have controlled their biological urges in this respect.

On a personal level one of the major risks taken during a career is, of course, to change jobs. Here the record clearly shows that we adhere to our biology. Studies have shown that women are far more loyal to an employer than men. Or, viewed another way, men are far more prone to risk a career move in order to gain the status and resources that their genes crave.

Apart from 'legitimate risk' taken in the course of one's job, there is, of course, 'illegal risk', that is, crime. Violent crime is overwhelmingly a male occupation. So it seems, in the world of business, is commercial fraud.

During the late 1980s, when I was first researching this book, the Anglo-Saxon world was coming to the end of an unprecedented peacetime economic boom. At such times there are generally a spate of financial scandals. (As Mark Twain observed: 'A crowded police court docket is the surest of all signs that trade is brisk and money plenty.') This time was no exception. Culprits of such scandals, from Ivan Boesky with his insider trading to Ernest Saunders and the 'Guinness Affair', were paraded in and out of court on the news, seemingly on a daily basis. I watched them all with interest. Every one was a man.

What drives rich, powerful and talented men like Boesky and Saunders to break the law? There seems no rational explanation for it. Perhaps the insatiable male desire to grab all the resources he can is a significant part of it. As John Stuart Mill observed: 'Men do not desire to be *rich*, but to be richer than other men.' This is entirely biological. Males of polygynous species attract mates by acquiring the most, not sufficient, resources.

2 AGGRESSION, DOMINANCE AND MALE HIERARCHIES

Our second prediction is that men will tend to try and dominate and be more aggressive, particularly to other men. This is how they are 'programmed' to acquire their unfair share of resources and thus mates.

Professor Richard Lynn (1991) of the University of Ulster conducted a massive study of work attitudes in nearly 14,000 university students across 43 countries. He was looking to see how work attitudes correlated with economic growth in these countries. His findings in this respect were fascinating (and we'll come back to them later in the book) but perhaps equally fascinating were the differences in attitudes between men and women.

Professor Lynn's study (1991) revealed the following:

> Some overall tendency for males to score more highly on competitiveness than females . . . a general trend for males to attach more value to money than females . . . an apparent tendency for males to have stronger preferences for those occupations which confer high financial rewards and power . . . Females showed stronger preferences for the caring professions.

Around the world, in every culture, we see this more aggressive attitude in males manifesting itself. For example, consider the ultimate act of aggression, murder: in the US 85 per cent of all murders are committed by men.

Men's tendency to dominate is also clear. The record clearly shows that, without exception, every single society has been controlled politically and economically by men. Today women rarely constitute more than five per cent of parliaments, for example, two per cent in the USA and, despite the example of Margaret Thatcher, three per cent in the UK.

Research shows that women generally think of themselves as less dominant than men and that they emit fewer dominance signals: not only physically – women are obviously smaller and have quieter, higher voices – but also behaviourally. For example women smile more and interrupt less often in conversation.

But the days when this proves a disadvantage to a career in business are ending. 'Animal' dominance is becoming a historical relic. Take the crudest most 'animal' form of achieving dominance: violence. Evidence clearly shows that today bullies have a very low place in modern society. Brawn is no longer an adequate means for success in the information age. So it is that, paradoxically, the natural urge of males to dominate and subjugate others is turning out to be, in some circumstances, a hindrance in actually achieving the status they crave.

Why? In the industrial age most workers were employed in tightly defined mass production jobs. What they had to do was precisely specified by management. The means to ensure that they did the right thing was a hierarchical management structure, borrowed from the military system. The management style was pure 'Theory X': workers were dominated by their superiors and were motivated by insecurity (another job was hard to come by) and fear. Of course the jobs were mind-numbingly boring. It's hard to think how an enlightened manager could have substituted 'job satisfaction' for coercion. (As W.H. Auden commented: 'One cannot walk through a mass production factory and not feel that one is in hell.') The system was designed and dominated by men. It still is where it exists today. Few women hold positions of power in established hierarchical organizations.

However, the modern business environment has changed. Modern workers in industry and commerce are decreasingly 'mass production' workers, controlled precisely by their superiors. They are what Peter Drucker has called 'knowledge workers'. They deal with ever-changing information that is so complex that the only people who can fully understand it are the workers themselves. Therefore they cannot be told exactly what to do: they cannot be 'outer-directed'; they have to be 'inner-directed'. They cannot be managed in the traditional sense. They have to be led: shown the goal of their efforts and motivated to use their knowledge, as only they know how, to that end. In this new world, management by dominance and fear are inappropriate. We've already seen how damaging stress caused by fear is to intellectual work. In any case, knowledge workers are valuable commodities and (with the underlying trends in demographics) about to become much more valuable and scarce. Such intelligent, sophisticated types, who can easily find work elsewhere, will not accept management by fear, or any other form of overt subjugation. They will (and particularly the good ones) vote with their feet in response to this sort of management.

The 'grateful society' is a thing of the past. The sophisticated modern workers see themselves as professionals and have to be treated with the sensitivity and respect that they can now command.

The male nature is not particularly well suited to this style of management. Men have to learn it. It comes much more readily to women. Indeed, studies show that the one difference in leadership style between men and women is women's greater concern and sensitivity for people and interpersonal issues. Exactly what is required of today's business leader.

Perhaps this is part of the reason why women seem to be succeeding in outflanking the traditional male hierarchies. Increasingly, women are establishing themselves as the new 'knowledge workers' and leaders of companies in the burgeoning information and services sector. In the USA 84 per cent of working women are now part of the information and services sectors.

As the world of commerce evolves into an area where knowledge and expertise increasingly dominate, so it appears to be becoming more attractive to women. Women graduate entries to commerce and industry are doubling every ten years in the USA and now stand at over one in four. Women are now earning one-third of the MBAs in the USA.

Sophisticated, information-intensive fledgling industries are also proving attractive to women. There have been great rises in the numbers of women entrepreneurs. In the UK recent reports show a 24 per cent increase in the number of women working for themselves. In the USA, two-thirds of all business startups are owned by women and the proportion of businesses owned and controlled by women is rising quickly.

So the pattern of male dominance in industry and commerce is changing. It is the USA which is in the vanguard of these changes: in manufacturing industry, where most of the old hierarchies persist, only 25 per cent of the top jobs are held by women, but overall, women now hold 40 per cent of the 14 million executive, administration and management jobs.

Unfortunately, notwithstanding the above, management is still associated with a male image in many quarters. Maleness (even if you are a female) can still open doors for you. Females in more masculine style of dress have a much better chance of being selected for management positions than those dressed in feminine styles. Male interviewers have been shown to prefer applicants (both male and female) who are not perfumed. Perhaps this is viewed as a more female trait. (Incidentally, female interviewers show the opposite inclination. It has been suggested that perhaps the best advice to interviewees is to carry perfume in your pocket and then squirt or don't squirt, as appropriate, once you determine the sex of your interviewer!)

Male hierarchies are not just hard on women. Around the world (and not just in business) established males give the up and coming generation of young men a hard time. The pattern is undeniable: seemingly pointless painful and dangerous initiations into 'manhood' occur in culture after culture – various forms of bodily mutilation abound, as do requirements to kill dangerous animals and perform dangerous tasks. In modern societies it is the young men who are generally required to serve in the armies. Why? Perhaps because, as with other polygynous animals, the older, established males want to hold on to the greater resources they have captured (for businessmen read higher position/salary) for as long as possible.

Many such organizations require their young managers to 'earn their spurs'. Often frequent relocations are imposed. Sometimes gruelling foreign postings are insisted upon. Often it seems that such companies are male dominated at the managerial level (Mars for example – a quasi-military regime if there ever was one). The justification for all this is, of course, the acquisition of requisite experience. There is no doubt more than a grain of truth in this. But could their male genes be helping them along for reasons of their own?

3   GUESS WHO'S LEFT HOLDING THE BABY?

Women will be more inclined to 'take care of the children'. There are animals, such as eagles, geese and foxes, who manage to live a truly monogamous life (an ideal which modern people aspire to but often fail to live up to). With both male and female parent animals restricted to the same limited number of offspring, you would expect both to be equally committed to caring for them. And this is exactly what we find.

With humans, however, a different situation exists. As we have seen, children are for women a low risk, moderate payoff investment: a woman has a few children and looks after them carefully to make sure that they survive. Men are inclined to seek high risk, high payoff investment and, if given the opportunity, are inclined to produce more children with more mates. The way to attract more mates is to amass more resources (in modern terms money) and so careers tend to come first.

There is another reason: women can be 100 per cent sure that their babies are *their* babies whereas men cannot ('mommy's babies daddy's maybes' goes the biologists' saying). A woman who devotes all her attention to her babies is certainly looking after offspring each of whom harbours 50 per cent of her own genes. If a man puts all his efforts into raising one set of offspring and has been the victim of infidelity, his efforts have all been in vain. Incidentally men's desire to turn 'daddy's maybes' into 'daddy's near certainties' explains such repugnant practices as Chinese foot binding, designed to restrict the mobility and chances of infidelity by wives.

Women's tendency to commit greater parental investment to their children is borne out by the fact that they have the prime child care role in every single human society. We are even aware of some of the mechanisms: it all seems to start with the action of the female hormone, prolactin, produced during lactation, on the brain. If you inject female rats with the stuff, it triggers nest building and similar caring activities. If you inject male rats with prolactin they do the same thing. But of course male rats don't normally produce prolactin themselves.

Even where humans have developed an ideological commitment to do it differently, as in some Israeli kibbutz, there has been a reversion to the 'biological norm', with women shouldering the main burden of child care.

Until recently in western countries, this burden of child rearing did not fall so fully upon the mother alone. She had her extended family, particularly the grand-parents, to lend a hand. It has been suggested that the reason that middle aged women pass through the menopause and lose their ability to have children is that the older they are the more likely it is that they will die during child birth. They can do more good promoting the future survival of their genes by not having any more children of their own, staying alive, and helping to look after their grandchildren (each of whom shares one-quarter of their genes).

With the mobility demanded by a modern business career this can leave modern mothers in an unenviable position: robbed of the support of an extended family and with a clash between her prime child-bearing years and prime career years. (It is estimated that in the USA 75 per cent of working women are in their prime child-bearing years.)

If we are to benefit from having talented mothers in the workforce, we will have to recognize the unnaturalness and unfairness of the present situation and lend them appropriate support. We shall soon be in desperate need of working mothers. This is not just because of the talents and qualities that women bring. We have a rapidly ageing population and a looming shortage of skilled workers. Any advanced country or business which cannot capitalize on this rich pool of talent is at a severe competitive disadvantage.

Enlightened governments have already woken up to the social and economic benefits of assisting the modern family with its child care needs. The picture is now quite clear: the more a state helps with child care the greater the proportion of mothers of young children in the workforce. The Scandinavian countries lead the way: Sweden requires that companies give a year's maternity leave at 90 per cent pay and provides state nurseries for most children over 18 months; nearly 90 per cent of Denmark's three to six year olds are in state nurseries. In these countries over 80 per cent of women with children aged below five are in the workforce. In backward Britain, which stands alone in having no statutory right to universal maternity leave (about half Britain's working mothers have not worked for their employers for more than two years and so do not qualify for the paltry six weeks at 90 per cent pay), less than half of women with children under five work.

Many companies too are realizing the economic benefits of attracting and keeping talented and valuable women workers by aiding with child care. Here the picture is somewhat different: direct aid through company crèches and the like is proving financially non-viable, but companies can and are helping through greater flexibility to allow working mothers to reconcile their family and work commitments – for example flexible leave policies and the provision of premises for commercial nurseries close to work. These companies are reaping the rewards.

4   WHY DON'T YOU SEE 'JONES & DAUGHTER LTD'?

Our fourth prediction is that wealth will tend to be left to males rather than females. This is not as intuitively obvious from our understanding of male and female biology. To understand why it should be so, consider the old investment adage: 'If you can't afford to lose you can't afford to win.' What this means is this: you have to be in a strong position to be able to take the risks necessary to get the big payoff. In humans the two sexes have, as we have seen, adopted differing investment strategies and to a large extent the same holds true.

If you are a parent at the bottom end of the social scale, you are unlikely to be able to give a son the sort of start in life that will propel him to the top where he can gather all the resources to attract the harem that he needs to get the big male payoff. Instead, because of his lowly caste, he's quite likely to remain single and fail to give any genetic return at all. This still seems to apply even today in advanced societies. For example in the USA the men who marry in a given year earn nearly 50 per cent more than those of the same age who do not.

Females are a better investment for parents at the bottom of the pecking order. It is a betting certainty that a daughter will find a mate. She doesn't need to amass resources; she just needs to be a nubile woman. Conversely sons are a much better bet for those at the top of the pile. Sons endowed with plenty of resources are likely to attract several mates.

There are many practices world-wide which reflect this. For example, female infanticide is common particularly among higher classes in many cultures. Male infanticide in lower classes is not reported, but it has been suggested that military service for the masses has the same effect!

The fact that men rich in women-attracting resources are likely to provide a better genetic payoff than women will explain to you why businesses and other forms of wealth have traditionally been left to the male line. There are countless businesses by such names as Jones and Son. Can you think of a single Jones and Daughter?

The sons seem every bit as aware of the biological importance of securing these resources. As Machiavelli commented four centuries ago: 'A son can bear with equanimity the loss of his father, but the loss of his inheritance may drive him to despair.'

Somehow (and the mechanism is not clear) the fact that males represent a better investment for the well off and females for the poor is even reflected in birth rates: couples at the top of the socioeconomic scale have male babies 52 per cent of the time whereas those at the bottom have female babies 52 per cent of the time. Furthermore if a woman experiences stress during pregnancy she is more likely to spontaneously abort a male baby than a female baby. Presumably her body recognizes that times are tough and that a high risk strategy is not appropriate.

5   THE MATING GAME

Our fifth prediction is that women will tend to 'marry up' (marry husbands wealthier than themselves) and men will tend to 'marry down' (marry wives less wealthy than themselves). This is because with all polygynous species females spend their efforts looking after children and not acquiring resources. A male looks for a female who shows signs that she will be a mother for his offspring. He will attract her by providing the necessary resources. It is therefore common in all polygynous species for the female to 'marry-up', to go to a mate with more resources than she has (the technical term is 'hypergynae').

This is exactly what we find with humans. You can observe the pattern: male doctors frequently marry female nurses, but the reverse is seldom seen; male bosses marry female secretaries and subordinates, but again the reverse is seldom seen. In the USA men at the top of the socioeconomic scale remain single only 5 per cent of the time, whereas those at the bottom remain single more than 30 per cent of the time.

This creates a problem for the modern successful woman: the higher up the socioeconomic scale, the more difficult it is for her to find someone to 'marry up' to. This explains in part why a disproportionately large number of successful women remain single.

We would not expect a man to look for the same traits in a woman; he wants to fertilize as many as possible and it is signs of reproductive potential that attract – looks, youth and so on. Not surprisingly, women spend more time and money on their appearance as is obvious to all (although research money has actually been invested in 'proving' this!).

It is important to note from the business perspective that this bias towards physical attractiveness in women spills over from dating into other areas. There is good evidence that physically attractive women are more persuasive as speakers. You can readily observe that most female sales representatives, news readers, advertising spokeswomen, and so on, have better than average looks.

There is another consequence of this difference in what men and women look for in a mate. Men mate when they have acquired the resources to attract a mate and women when they are at their peak child-bearing and raising capacity. It is not surprising then that men marry later than women and that 'December–May marriages' are common (but only with the man December and the woman May) and that bosses (typically successful and resource rich) and secretaries (typically young and nubile) so frequently indulge in liaisons!

IN CONCLUSION

We have suggested in this chapter that our evolutionary history makes men more inclined to aggressive, domineering, acquisitive behaviour and women more inclined to caring behaviour. The chapter started with me leaning over backwards to reassure readers that a chapter on sex was not going to be sexist. Everyone associates sexism with unfair criticism of women. However, if this chapter has been critical of a sex, it has been critical of men.

We have seen on several occasions how, particularly in the modern, sophisticated business environment, primeval aggressive 'male behaviour' is inappropriate. The truth of this is perhaps emphasized most strongly by the futility of military service as a training for business. The military is unquestionably the most 'male' of all institutions. Military experience was a useful grounding for the old industries that were, after all, modelled on the military. But today, as Peter Drucker (1986) has asserted:

> The much vaunted skills which a military teaches – the benefits of military service as proclaimed by every recruiting poster – are only of the most limited value to the civilian economy. A year or two of community service for

young people would have greater value both to them and to society than two years in the barracks.

Some people have gone further. It has been suggested that men, with their programmed propensity for self-aggrandisement and ruthless male–male competition, are unworthy candidates for leadership of nations with the capability to destroy the planet. Perhaps it would be better left to the sex more concerned with investing in life?

But nothing is all bad! As we will see later there is a link between competitiveness and economic success. And as we have already seen, competitiveness is one ingredient that males certainly bring to businesses. It is a question of harnessing this and curbing the more destructive excesses of male behaviour. As my wife tells me: men have to become more like women and women more like men.

IN SUMMARY

WHAT HAVE WE LEARNT?

No one should deny that men and women are *equal*: equal in terms of worth and equal in terms of their right to realize their full potential. But this doesn't mean that they are *identical*. Evolution has equipped men and women with radically different bodies. It seems inconceivable that it would have provided identical minds. All the evidence suggests that men and women are *inclined* (not compelled!) to behave differently.

Generally, in the animal kingdom, males and females adopt differing strategies for maximizing their fitness (passing on as many genes as possible to the next generation). Females generally take the 'bank deposit' approach: they have a few babies (modest return) which they nurture to give them the best chance of surviving (modest risk). Males, on the other hand, generally take the 'venture capital' approach: they try to have many babies with numerous females (high return), but are very likely to end up having none (high risk), because all the other males are following the same approach.

Generally then male animals are polygynous (they try to have several mates) and to achieve this they adopt an aggressive and risky approach to life. There is much evidence that humans follow this general pattern (and that monogamy – one wife – is a recent social invention). This allows us to explain various facets of male and female behaviour, particularly in business.

Men have a greater propensity to take rash risks. Men are more aggressive and domineering and tend to rise to the top of old-fashioned hierarchical organizations. Men are less inclined to take their fair share of parental responsibility. Men tend to leave their businesses to their sons rather than to their daughters – because their evolutionary wisdom tells them that there is no limit to the number of children that a resource rich male can have.

WHAT CAN WE DO ABOUT IT?

○   Your sex is one more reason why you shouldn't trust your intuition where risk is concerned. Beware of reckless risk taking by men.

○   Aim for the Japanese and German attitude. They manage to retain the more positive male traits such as competitiveness, while curbing the propensity for rash risk taking.

○   If you're a woman, look to a career outside an old fashioned, male dominated, hierarchical organization (if you must work in one, adopt a masculine style). Instead, target a modern organization in the information or services sector where talent and not politics is more important.

○   Modern companies and economies need talented women. It must be economic to help with child care.

○   Don't feel that you are a slave to the inclinations that your sex saddles you with. With a little self-discipline you can override them.

6

CO-OPERATION
and how to harness it

❖

J.Z. Young, one of the great commentators on the human animal, bravely suggested our most important asset as a species:

> So far as we can plan, we should do so on the basis that man's special genius is for co-operation. This is not simply optimism, as some people seem to wish to show, but a rational forecast based upon the evidence. Men and women have tendencies to love and help much more than to hate each other: we are not fallen angels but risen apes, getting better!

> (Young, 1979)

And nowhere do we *need* to get better at co-operating more than in business. Co-operation is vital to success in a modern business.

Jeffrey Pfeffer (1992), a professor at Stanford business school, in his book *Managing with Power* reckons that as organizations have become flatter and employees 'empowered' and informed, the traditional levers of power (such as control of budgets and information and formal power) are becoming ineffective. Effective managers now have to campaign rather than coerce, to communicate rather than mandate, to co-operate rather than dominate.

Fortunately, people have an insatiable need to socialize and to co-operate. This certainly extends to the workplace. We simply have to learn how to harness it.

Studies show that new entrants to companies spend huge amounts of time seeking out social support. Those who cannot find support and friendship in the work setting are more prone to mental health problems – anxiety, depression, somatic symptoms, low self-esteem and low subjective competence.

'Sociality' seems to be as important to us as eating and drinking. It is in our blood, or rather genes. But why should it be? What was in it for our genes to have learnt to co-operate?

WHY ARE WE SO PRONE TO CO-OPERATE?

Once we adapted a hunter–gatherer lifestyle on the African savannah, hunting was our way of life. We needed to belong to an effective group to hunt and to defend ourselves against other groups of humans and animals such as lions and hyenas.

But we did not simply evolve a vague 'be nice to others' inclination. We must co-operate to survive but our genes ensure that it is strictly along lines that are in their best interests. There are various forces driving the way that we work together in groups and we shall look at the first of these, altruism, in this chapter. The others we will come to in later chapters.

In an attempt to understand what altruism is and how and why it works, let's first of all take a foray into the familiar world of business. Imagine a company facing troubled times. Insolvency looms and the company turns to its bank for help. A loan doesn't look like a sensible proposition by all the normal lending criteria of banks. Nevertheless, the bank goes ahead with the loan. The company pulls through and the bank makes a little money out of the loan, but an amount which is disproportionately small when compared to the risk that it took. The bank seems to have behaved altruistically. Altruism is where someone engages in an act which is likely to do someone else good but himself or herself harm.

This sort of behaviour would threaten the basis of free market capitalism: the selfish behaviour of many individuals summing together to act as the 'invisible hand' establishing economic prices for all products and commodities and redirecting capital and resources to ensure that they are used in the most efficient manner, producing what is wanted at the most economic price. Companies that are not economic should go to the wall, so that the resources can be put to more productive use. The key concept here is that individuals are supposed to act selfishly; otherwise the whole system breaks down.

How could the bank behave like this and remain true to the free market economy, acting in its own economic interests to maximize its competitiveness and efficiency? Well, this hypothetical exchange took place in Germany and in Germany banks often hold large equity stakes in companies (quite unlike banks in Anglo-Saxon countries). The bank in question owned a large proportion of the stock in the troubled company and it reasoned that a moderate loan, while somewhat risky, was a good business proposition given the very large losses that it would make if the company became insolvent. The bank was in fact acting out of pure selfishness. The foundations of capitalism seem secure once more and Adam Smith can rest in peace.

As genuinely altruistic behaviour between businesses would threaten the basis of a true free market economy, so the existence of altruism between individual animals and people seemed for a long time to threaten the basis of evolutionary theory.

Evolution is, as we have seen, concerned with the survival of the fittest. The fittest individual is the one who manages to pass the most copies of his or her genes on to the next generation. The next generation then contains a greater proportion of these genes and the species contains more of the traits that the genes produce.

However, in another scenario, a small child runs out in front of a bus and an adult, without thinking, dashes out, putting himself in considerable danger, to save the child. Such commendable feats of altruism regularly appear in our newspapers. But surely if we are products of evolution they shouldn't. Surely the adult is increasing the child's fitness at the expense of his own: the child is more likely to live, reproduce and pass on copies of his genes as a result of this intervention and the adult is less likely to live, reproduce and pass on copies of his genes.

There are even more bizarre examples of altruism to be found in the animal kingdom. Particularly among the 'social insects', for example the ants, and termites. Among these insects we find weird and wonderful creatures who are perfectly sterile and who seem to have given up their lives and any prospect of reproducing for the good of others. David Barash (1981) has described some of these curiosities as follows:

> enormous soldiers with mouth parts so specialised for warfare that they cannot feed themselves and must be fed by other specialised workers; other 'nasute' soldiers that are walking squirt guns, generating a stream of irritating or sticky fluid; 'repletes' that serve as living storage tanks of nutrient fluids; and members of certain termite castes, the geometric shape of whose heads precisely matches the entrance to their hive where they obediently stand as living doors, moving aside only when they receive an appropriate knock from a colleague.

If there were a gene for altruism, it would surely result in each generation containing fewer and fewer copies of itself. (Its bearers would keep sacrificing themselves until there was not a single gene for altruism left.) Surely genes for behaviour such as altruism are self-eliminating!

For this reason, for many years the existence of altruism was a thorn in the side of the modern theory of evolution. Then, in the early 1960s a young research student by the name of William Hamilton pulled all the pieces of an explanation together. At first his reasoning was not well accepted; in fact he was told that his work was not up to the standards of the University of London and that he could not receive his Ph.D. In order to gain employment he rushed out a paper called 'The genetical evolution of social behaviour', a paper which was to prove to be one of the most important advances in our understanding of evolution since Darwin's *The Origin of Species.*

The title of the paper may lead you to suppose that the explanation that Hamilton proffered was frighteningly technical and complicated. It wasn't: all he really proposed was that people (and animals) behave altruistically for essentially the same reason that the bank did in the example that opened this chapter. The difference being that where the bank acted to help the other company because it contained some of the bank's money, people (or animals) help other people because they contain some of their genes.

A person's genes do not exist solely inside himself. They exist in many other individuals too. For example, if he has a child, then copies of half his genes will exist inside his child. (You will recall that a child receives half his genes from his father and the other half from his mother.) Similarly he will share half his genes with a brother or sister. A more distant relative will share less of his genes; a grandchild for example will receive a quarter of his genes (a half of the half of his genes carried by his child).

Just as our bank could help itself by assisting another company that contained some of its money, so a person can help his fitness by assisting someone who contains some copies of his genes. Furthermore, just as the bank will be more inclined to help and take risk for a company depending upon just how much of its money the company possesses, so a person is more likely to be altruistic to a close relative (who contains copies of many of his genes) than a distant relative (who contains few).

The logical conclusion of this argument is summed up in the following story. J.B.S. Haldane was once asked whether he would give up his life for his brother. He replied that he would not. But he would give up his life for three brothers . . . or nine cousins . . . His reason was, of course, that three brothers would contain more copies of his genes than his own body did (one and a half times as many to be precise) as would nine cousins (who would contain one and an eighth times as many).

IT ALL SEEMS TO BE 'RELATIVE'

It is not surprising, then, that we humans are obsessed with identifying our relatedness to others. Every single language contains a vast vocabulary of words conveying blood relationships between individuals: son, daughter, mother, father, brother, sister, aunt, uncle, cousin, half cousin, great aunt and so on and so forth. We all take it for granted that we should know our close relatives. Now it becomes apparent why: just as our bank keeps a careful ledger of where its money is tied up, so we are locating where the most copies of our genes are to be found.

And around the world you can observe practices which are clearly nothing more than people discriminating in favour of their own genes. In Australia when a stranger arrived at an aboriginal settlement, he was quizzed on his genealogy. If he was somehow related to someone in the village he was welcomed, if not he was killed. There is an old Arab proverb: 'Me against my brother, me and my brother and my cousins against my friends; me, my brother, cousins and friends against our enemies in the village; all of these and the whole village against the next village . . . '

Shouldn't we expect that in order for people to work unselfishly together they should be closely related? Well certainly, in days gone by when earning a living was more of a life and death business, this was often the case. The Baring Sea Eskimos hunt the bowhead whales from open skin-covered boats. As you can imagine it is a dangerous affair. An observer noted in 1969: 'In days past the old people strongly urged that a man hunt only with his relatives, because if the boat got into trouble out on the ice a nonclansman would be less prone to help a man out of difficulty' (C. Hughes 1960).

So far it seems clear cut: the more closely related two people are the more they will be inclined to work unselfishly together. But in practice it's not so simple. To understand why you have to understand the ways in which people have evolved to recognize their relatives. Obviously the best way would be to have some physical way of recognizing kin. Some animals seem to have evolved such a mechanism. Ground squirrels will be kinder to siblings than to non-siblings. Even if you separate two siblings at birth and raise them apart with other non-related squirrels, when you put the siblings together again, they will be less aggressive and more helpful to their sibling than the squirrels with whom they have been raised. Somehow, perhaps by smell, they can tell where most copies of their genes are to be found and they look after them accordingly.

It seems that we humans never had to evolve such an ability. True we can tell that people of other races are not related to us (and here, unfortunately, is a biological basis for racism) but for our own race, apart from the use of language in modern times, we have no way of telling whether someone is closely related or not. It seems that we never evolved such an ability because there was no need. When the human tendencies for altruism were evolving we were almost certainly living in small bands of 50 or less, roaming a range of a couple of thousand square kilometres – about the same as a wolf pack does – on the African savannahs. The emergence of weapons must have created very strong pressures for the evolution of co-operation and altruism. Tribes that didn't co-operate effectively would have been wiped out by those that did. We could tell our brothers and sisters, we were raised by the same mother, and the rest of the band, because of its small size, must also have been quite closely related to us. We recognized our kin as the other members of our troop: the people we lived and worked with, who shared the troop's customs and dialect.

This was enough to allow us to identify and look after people who held copies of our genes. But suddenly we invented agriculture and this allowed much larger settlements to develop. In these larger groupings technology and civilization rapidly developed and we soon found ourselves in today's modern societies. Here the people we live among and work among are probably not our close relatives, but our biology has not had time to catch up with these explosive social changes and now, as we shall see, it is often fooled.

If there are people with whom we live and work and who are suitably similar to ourselves in their customs, their accents, the way they dress and so forth, then our biological programming assumes that they are probably relatives and we tend to be more altruistic towards them. As we saw this was a good guide when this tendency evolved in our ancestors as they roamed in small bands on the African savannahs, and so the genes of people who behaved altruistically according to this rule of thumb really did do better, the genes became more and more widespread and so did the behaviour.

You should now begin to understand the strength of the old school tie network, the university alumni network and many others. The members of these groups 'accidentally' treat each other as relatives. Perhaps it is significant that the USA, a country made up of many vastly different groups of immigrants is the most 'go-getting' and aggressive of societies. Perhaps the obvious differences between people encourage a more selfish society.

These differences between people and the effects they have on co-operation are of vital concern to businesses. As commerce becomes more and more global, enlightened multinational companies are staffing their boards and headquarters with an ethnic diversity that mirrors their global marketplace. Firms are on the look out for the Euro-manager who is as comfortable doing business in Cologne as in Coventry. This encourages a broad outlook and avoids the 'group-think' that a mono-cultural group can so easily fall into.

So goes the theory. But is it right? To answer the question, Warren Watson, a professor at the University of North Texas, and colleagues recently performed an experiment (Watson *et al.* 1993). They studied the behaviour of nearly 200 business students who organized into either culturally diverse or culturally homogeneous teams to solve business case studies. The teams met only four times. On each occasion they worked for one hour on a specific case study.

Counterintuitively, the culturally homogeneous groups outperformed the culturally diverse groups on all occasions. However, while they were markedly better at the first two case studies, they were only marginally better than the culturally diverse groups at the last two. Furthermore, by the end of the experiment, the diverse groups were more creative than the homogeneous group, looking at problems more broadly and considering more alternative solutions.

Nevertheless, one can't help drawing the somewhat distasteful conclusion, that, at least in the short term, similar people co-operate better.

So powerful is this tendency to favour people who are similar (and possibly therefore related to us) that experimenters have shown with school children that by arbitrarily choosing and focusing on a simple trait which some of the children have and others do not, such as blue eyes, they can easily divide the children into camps with strong co-operation within and conflict between them.

Thus we effectively have modern tribes. Garrett Hardin (1972) has defined a modern tribe as follows:

> Any group of people that perceives itself as a distinct group, and is so perceived by the outside world, may be called a tribe. The group might be a race, as ordinarily defined, but it need not be; it can just as well be a religious sect, a political group, or an occupational group. The essential characteristic of a tribe is that it should follow a double standard of morality – one kind of behaviour for in-group relations, another for out-group
>
> It is one of the unfortunate and inescapable characteristics of tribalism that it eventually evokes counter tribalism (or, to use a different figure of speech, it 'polarizes' society).

Many facets of the business world now begin to fall into place.

Peters and Waterman in their classic *In Search of Excellence* (1981) noted that a strong value-driven culture was one of the characteristics of excellent companies. Is not this common way of doing things all part of forming a strongly bonded modern tribe and is not the modern business the main outlet for our ancient tribal inclinations?

Now you can begin to comprehend the intense rivalry and hostility between competing sales regions at the annual conference. (As Bertand Russell said: 'Few people can be happy unless they hate some other person, nation or creed.')

Perhaps you acknowledge why people group together in organizations such as the Institute of Directors and the freemasons. You begin to see a new significance in the old school tie. These are all manifestations or manipulations of our tendency to behave altruistically to those we perceive as being from the 'same tribe'.

Often these days the altruism is 'inappropriate': we are in no way related to our ex-school chums. But our genes are a long way from catching up with this reality.

The other way that we can be fooled into being 'inappropriately' altruistic is when people make allusions by means of language to kinships that don't really exist. When you think about this they're very common. In the trade union movement, for example, where the membership show solidarity by referring to each other as 'brothers'. Think of national leaders eliciting national co-operation by talk of the 'motherland'; think of religious organizations where the members are all referred to by terms indicating kinship – 'father' and so on; think of people securing help for their offspring by non-kin through inviting them to become 'godparents'. How often have you heard firms espousing a 'family atmosphere'. It seems that even talk of kinship can goad people into altruism.

But the degree, or rather perceived degree, that one person is related to another isn't the only factor that determines whether or not he will behave altruistically. He is not solely concerned with the likely benefit to the copies of his genes in the body of the recipient of his altruism, but also to the cost to himself and the genes within himself.   This is why appeals to people's generosity often stress the small cost involved. The more distant and less related the beneficiary, the more this is stressed: 'Only one dollar provides milk for a month,' for example.

The cost of being altruistic is not, however, constant throughout a person's life: a young person, who has the bearing and rearing of his own children before him, has much to lose if he puts himself at a disadvantage for someone else's benefit and so young people are less prone to altruism; an old person, who has already had and reared his own children, has very little to lose and so he is much more inclined to altruism. Which explains why in business organizations we associate aggressive, iconoclastic behaviour from the young (recall the expression 'Young Turks') and why many older managers become known as mentors and 'Father Figures'. It also explains why the advertising industry has learnt that advertising encouraging altruistic behaviour (most notably for charities) is more effective when targeted at a mature audience.

And so we have seen that all altruism is in fact an attempt at selfishness. Sometimes, for example because evolution has not caught up with social changes, it is 'misdirected' but the intention of our evolved tendencies is always selfishness. As mentioned earlier, business and the whole free market system is about selfishness, about each individual driving the best bargain for himself and in the process producing the most economic use of capital and factors. The two appear to be well aligned, unless, that is, one tries to do business with a relative. Then one can imagine an uncomfortable conflict between wanting to drive the best bargain for the business and wanting to help a relative. Perhaps this explains the old adage: 'Never do business with a relative.'

IS IT REALLY ALL RELATIVE?

You may, by now, be forgiven for drawing the conclusion that the only time that people will assist others is when they believe that they are assisting a relative who harbours copies of their own genes. This isn't actually the case.

Let's return to our German bank. It doesn't only lend money to companies in whom it has an equity stake. It will lend money to any business, provided that it is convinced that the interest repayments that it requires to make a profit will be met. And a company doesn't borrow money from the bank for the purpose of paying the bank interest; it does so because it believes it can put the money to work, pay back the bank and still make a profit. The bank and the company are both acting out of self-interest, but by co-operating they both help each other and themselves. This form of co-operation is called reciprocity: one party assists the other (the bank lends the company the money that it needs to run its business) in the expectation that the other will assist it (the company will pay back the money with interest).

Reciprocity is an important concept in business and it is often taught to people who are learning good 'team work' by means of a game called 'The Prisoner's Dilemma'. The game goes like this.

You are one of two prisoners. You have been accused of committing a crime in complicity with the other prisoner. If neither of you confesses to the crime and neither of you implicates the other you will both be released. There is a reward for mutual co-operation and you score 2 points.

But if you implicate the other prisoner, provided he or she doesn't implicate you, you will be released and given a reward. So there is a temptation to defect from co-operating and profit from the even higher payoff and, if you carry it off successfully, you score 3 points.

If, however you defect to attempt to gain this bumper payoff and the other prisoner, in trying to do the same thing, implicates *you*, you will both be put in jail. So mutual defection is punished and, in the game, you score only 1 point.

Finally, if you set out to co-operate with your partner and do not implicate him or her, but he or she selfishly and successfully acquires the big payoff of release and the reward by implicating you, then you are given an even heavier jail sentence than if you had both implicated each other – after all it appears that you alone were responsible for this crime. The payoff for being the scapegoat is the worst of all and you score no points.

You can see the dilemma. Co-operating will get you a reasonable payoff but you are encouraged to defect and implicate the other prisoner for two reasons: first, you are tempted to defect, implicate the other prisoner and abscond with freedom and the reward; second, you're worried that if you do co-operate, the other prisoner will succumb to temptation, take off with freedom and the reward and leave you with an even heavier jail sentence than if you'd both defected. What to do?

Well, researchers in biology have been very interested in the answer to that question as this simple little game in many ways mirrors the dilemma facing people and animals when they decide whether to co-operate or act selfishly. Mutual co-operation may be beneficial but it's better if you can coerce someone into helping you and manage not to return the favour, and it's better not to co-operate than to expend the effort of doing a favour that isn't returned. Thus the genes which encouraged their bearers to play the game in the most advantageous way will have been at a survival advantage and we can expect that the most effective strategy for playing this game will mirror the most effective strategy for co-operation in life.

So, a super tournament was arranged by a researcher called Robert Axelrod (1984). Fourteen experts in a branch of mathematics called 'game theory', which is concerned with just this sort of thing, submitted their strategies for playing 200 consecutive games of 'The Prisoner's Dilemma'. Some of the strategies, as you might expect, were extremely complicated and esoteric. The strategies were programmed into the computer and each strategy was pitted against all the others. Surprisingly the simplest strategy submitted achieved the highest average score. It is a strategy known as 'tit-for-tat' and it operates like this: as an opening move you co-operate; from then on you do whatever your opponent did for his or her last move. This means that as long as an opponent co-operates you will always continue to co-operate and never cheat. However, as soon as your opponent cheats you will strike back on the next move and continue to do so until he or she again co-operates; but as soon as co-operation is resumed you will always reward this by co-operating yourself.

To provide a still stiffer test for this simple strategy, Axelrod circulated the results of the tournament and invited entries for another tournament. This time there were 62 entries each forewarned about the success of the 'tit-for-tat' strategy. Once again, despite all the sophisticated attempts to better it, no strategy could produce a better average score than the simple 'tit-for-tat'.

Axelrod then mimicked evolution by running further rounds of the competition with the least successful strategies being removed at the end of each round. Even as the less successful strategies were removed 'tit-for-tat' continued to fare the best and eventually it displaced all the other strategies. Encouraged by these results Axelrod and his co-worker Hamilton were able to *prove* that there is no better strategy than 'tit-for-tat': one should never be the first to defect; one should defect only in retaliation when one's partner has defected first; and one should be forgiving after only one act of defection. In summary one should be ever the optimist: always co-operating unless one's partner defects and always being forgiving at the first sign of co-operation.

It appears that our genes have learnt this lesson too. We have a powerful set of emotions which, when you think about it, encourage us to adopt this ever-optimistic, enlightened and most effective 'tit-for-tat' strategy in our dealings with others.

When someone does us a favour we have a natural feeling of gratitude; we are encouraged by our genes to pay it back, to play 'tit-for-tat'. Interestingly, when our tendency towards co-operation was evolving, food was much prized and could not be taken for granted as it is today. Food sharing would have been a particularly powerful favour and our genes may still reflect this; the buying of lunch is a common way to establish a business relationship to this day. Perhaps this ritual, which seems to have an inexplicable significance, now makes a little more sense. It has been pointed out that money is a formalized system of reciprocity: you obtain it in return for giving up some of your belongings or efforts and it entitles you to buy a corresponding amount of property or the fruits of other people's efforts.

When someone fails to pay back a favour or lets down a friend we have a natural feeling of moral outrage; we are encouraged by our genes to punish them, to play 'tit-for-tat'. If we let people down we feel a sense of guilt; we are not playing 'tit-for-tat' and our genes don't like it, they encourage us to return to the proven optimal strategy. Indeed without a sense of these moral values the whole 'tit-for-tat' foundation of our society would break down and, as Norman Dixon (1988) has pointed out: 'Without this capacity every other person would have to be a policeman and all the rest venereologists.'

Many of the non-verbal signals for friendship and liking can be seen as an invitation to play 'tit-for-tat'. For example, more self-disclosure during conversation (giving information about oneself in return for like from the other) and touching the other (possibly a relic from the reciprocal grooming that is so important in binding primate groups together).

And 'tit-for-tat' *is* the best strategy, but only when the number of games to be played is sufficiently high. If you watch contestants playing 'The Prisoner's Dilemma' you will see that even those who tend to adopt a 'tit-for-tat' strategy tend to depart from it as the series of games that they are playing draws to a close; people begin to cheat more often. If you are only going to play one round of the game, the best strategy is to default, not to co-operate.

So it is in life: what's the point in doing someone a favour if you're never going to see them again in order for them to repay it? What's the harm in fleecing someone if they're not going to be around to retaliate in the future? Perhaps this explains the business saying 'bargain like a Gypsy, but pay like a gentleman'. A Gypsy is itinerant; he is less likely to meet someone again, so he is less interested in 'tit-for-tat'. He will drive a harder bargain. A gentleman is established in a community. He needs goodwill. He needs to play 'tit-for-tat'. So he will be a better payer.

If you want to engender co-operation in an organization you will need to ensure that people are going to interact often enough for them to expect that when they do a favour it will be paid back, for them to start adopting a 'tit-for-tat' strategy.

There are two factors which can help bring this about. First, turnover in jobs should not be too fast to allow people the time to start playing 'tit-for-tat'. Not surprisingly, companies with high turnovers tend to have lower morale and team spirit.

Second, the size of an organization should be kept down. We're all famil-iar with the modern realization that 'small is beautiful' and that activities should be decentralized and hived off to small autonomous units. When huge organizations mean that people interact very infrequently the prospects for a healthy game of 'tit-for-tat' developing of course are greatly reduced.

Another reason why co-operation is hard to elicit in large, diffuse organi-zations is called by economists the 'tragedy of the commons'. To explain this, imagine you work in a small factory with three cost centres. You run one of them. You are paid a bonus based on the overall performance of the factory. Cutting your costs is unpleasant, but as one of only three cost cen-tres, it's worth your while because your performance has a major effect on the factory's performance.

Now imagine you're part of a large factory running one of 30 cost centres. Cost cutting by you will have a negligible effect on total costs. Why go through the pain? Why bother? The trouble is that everyone else feels that way too. Hence everyone suffers. Hence the 'tragedy of the commons'.

Therefore to encourage the development of co-operation ensures that people are working together in smallish groups for longish periods of time giving them plenty of opportunity to reciprocate.

In the USA there has of late been a trend towards the use of 'super teams'. These are 'self-managing' groups of workers who have proven that they can produce superior results through self-arranged co-operation than were pre-viously achieved by diktat from layers of middle managers. But these 'super teams' do not succeed in any circumstance. The May 1990 cover story in *Fortune* pointed out: 'They make sense only when a job entails a high level of dependency among three or more people.' Exactly the conditions we have defined for a good game of 'tit-for-tat' to flourish.

Don't underestimate the time that it can take for co-operation to take root.

In January 1987, John Neill led an employee buy-out of Britain's Unipart – a spare parts firm for cars. He was advised at the time that its manufacturing operation was an intractable mess and should be closed down. But Mr Neill believed that he could import Japanese working methods, such as Total Quality. So, he sent a work party to Japan to learn these techniques. They succeeded and returned home charged with enthusiasm. Only to run into a brick wall of non-acceptance in the factory back at home. Rather than throwing in the towel, John Neill had them establish their new working practices in a corner of the factory. 'They became missionaries', he says. Once the methods had been proved to the rest of the workforce, Neill was confident to give their wholesale introduction another try. It worked. Piecework rates were abandoned in favour of ability related pay; production was reorganized through the introduction of small, flexible teams; seven layers of management was cut down to three; new equipment was installed; faster set-up times were established; costs tumbled by £2m pounds per year.

Roger Ball, the factory's general manager, summed it all up as 'releasing talent already there on the shopfloor'.

1991 was the British motor industry's worst ever year with corporate losses of many millions. But Unipart increased its pre-tax profits by 18 per cent to over £15m.

CO-OPERATION ISN'T ALWAYS GOOD

The development of co-operation can have powerful benefits between co-workers, but perhaps there are other circumstances when the development of reciprocity might not be quite so pleasing. I'm thinking of the development of co-operation between supposed competitors. To understand how this can take place, consider a piece of history from the First World War.

Unbelievable as it is, during this most bloody of conflicts, with all its carnage and the loss of millions of lives, there was actually co-operation between the opposing forces. The First World War was a prime 'breeding ground' for reciprocity, for the giving and returning of favours: it was a war of attrition with men closely lined up in opposing trenches for long periods of time. Just the sort of conditions where we expect co-operation to flourish. And flourish it did.

Co-operation was not just restricted to the well known cease-fires on Christmas Day; it went much, much further. Provided the other side did the same, troops would shoot to miss. Officers courtmartialled large numbers of troops, but still the co-operation flourished. The masquerade of combat became more sophisticated. Artillery would be fired to land in the same place at the same time every day, allowing troops to appear to take risks that didn't really exist. It has been estimated that at times up to one-third of all British troops were engaged in this sort of 'live and let live' relationship with the enemy. The solution proved to be raiding attacks by up to 200 men to kill the enemy in their trenches. There was no way that a pact could operate under these circumstances. You couldn't fake a raid. Raids provoked counter raids and the whole system broke down.

It's maybe not such a good idea to have your managers liaise too closely and too often with the competition. Perhaps the same sort of thing can develop. An example of the dangers of co-operation between competitors who are in regular close contact is given by John Burke, former chairman of Glaxo pharmaceuticals, in his book *The Management of Luck*:

> By pact mentality, I mean mutual cover-up. 'If you don't question or raise this, I won't question or raise that.' The biggest culprits in my experience are associations of managers. Like penguins, we all turn up to meetings and walk around in circles to keep each other warm. 'We can't do anything about exports', we chant. 'The pound is too strong.' We can all report back to our respective bosses that everyone is in the same boat.
> 'Sorry, sir, but it's all the fault of the pound.'
> 'Are you sure?'
> 'Absolutely. I was down at this meeting yesterday . . . '

It seems then reciprocity is not all good. Possibly the most important and controversial manifestation of reciprocity in business is in the interests of the business, if not of society as a whole. It is collusion between businesses. As long ago as 1776 Adam Smith in the immortal *Wealth of Nations* made his famous observation: 'People of the same trade seldom meet together, even for merriment and diversion, but the conversation ends in a conspiracy against the public, or in some contrivance to raise prices.'

Surely this is a manifestation of our instinct for reciprocity, for playing 'tit-for-tat'. Of course, in advanced industrial countries these days, such overt collusion is forbidden by antitrust laws and, although you still read of the occasional case, it is not highly prevalent.

Such is our inclination to reciprocity, though, that it doesn't stop collusion, tacit or unspoken collusion, occurring all the time. Tacit collusion doesn't break out in monopolies – there's no one to collude with – and it tends not to break out when there are many small firms all competing fiercely with each other (this comes close to what the textbook calls perfect competition and, as the label suggests, firms tend to compete under such circumstances – it's just inconceivable that so many small firms could come to an unspoken understanding).

In between these two polar extremes we have what is known as an 'oligopoly', an industry dominated by a few key players. You will recall from earlier in this chapter the circumstances under which reciprocity tends to 'break out' among people – it's when they know that they are going to interact frequently, so that if they do a favour it will be paid back and if they 'pull a fast one' they will be retaliated against. These are exactly the circumstances that companies in oligopolies operate in. They will, for example, find themselves in competition with the same few companies in tender after tender.

The example of General Electric and Westinghouse in the large turbine generator business is a case in point. Back in 1963 demand in the USA for large turbine generators had collapsed and Westinghouse and General Electric (GE) were fighting to survive in the business. Things looked bleak. Most sales were to private electricity companies. Although both GE and Westinghouse had published book prices for their generators, the actual bid price was the result of a secret discount and the loser was never told what the winning bid was.

General Electric proved to be a master player of 'tit-for-tat'. You will remember the basic tenet of 'tit-for-tat': as an opening move you co-operate; from then on you do whatever your opponent did for his last move. This means that as long as an opponent co-operates you will always continue to co-operate and never cheat. But as soon as your opponent cheats you will strike back on the next move and continue to do so until he again co-operates; but as soon as he co-operates you will always reward this by co-operating yourself.

As an opening move GE co-operated. It actually published, in the trade press for Westinghouse to see, a simplified price list with an announcement that they would in future bid to all customers at book price times a multiple *and they announced that multiple* to be 0.76. A classic invitation to play 'tit-for-tat'.

Sure enough within days Westinghouse had withdrawn its own price list and begun using the GE price list with a multiplier of – you guessed it – 0.76.

All went well through 1963 and into 1964. Westinghouse continued in this manner and accordingly GE held to its price list and its published multiple until in 1964 when it felt that Westinghouse had engaged in secret price cutting. GE immediately cut its multiple, thus lowering the price of its generators and 'punishing' Westinghouse.

Westinghouse soon saw the folly of its ways. It circulated rumours around the industry that its price cutting was actually as a result of a misinterpretation of GE's book. Westinghouse realized how beneficial 'tit-for-tat' was for it so it also announced a price increase, published a list of its orders and bids and instituted a price protection clause which would penalize Westinghouse if it cut prices again in the future.

GE again played the master tit-for-tatter and raised its multiplier to the Westinghouse level and, with Westinghouse now educated in the wisdom of co-operating, the same multiplier remained throughout the 1960s and 1970s.

All this without a single explicit word about co-operation.

GE and Westinghouse is a typical example of behaviour frequently occurring in oligopolies. A whole branch of microeconomics, known as 'The New Industrial Economics', has sprouted from the now classic book *The Strategy of Conflict* (Schelling, 1960), which looks at this sort of interaction between companies. And more recently Michael Porter in his 1980 book, *Competitive Strategy*, cited methods for effectively encouraging your competitor to play 'tit-for-tat'. (For example, the 'cross parry': establish a presence in **his** major market so that if he comes into **your** major market and starts doing nasty things, like price cutting, you can pay him back in kind and encourage him to return to the cosier status quo ante.)

Does the need for such extensive and highly policed antitrust laws and the existence of such an elaborate academic analysis of tacit collusion stem, at least in part, from our biological inclination towards reciprocity, towards playing 'tit-for-tat'?

IN SUMMARY

WHAT HAVE WE LEARNT?

Co-operation is, perhaps, our most important asset. It is a deep rooted part of human nature. Co-operation is more vital than ever in today's non-hierarchical organizations. The old levers of power – like control of budgets, control of information and formal power – are vanishing. Effective managers today *must* elicit co-operation.

But, paradoxically, our inclinations to co-operate and help others evolved for purely selfish reasons. People will only co-operate when they 'think', deep down, that they are helping their own 'fitness'.

The first type of co-operation is 'altruism'. This is when someone helps someone else apparently to his or her own detriment. The reason that people are inclined to do this is that copies of our genes are found not only in our own bodies but also in our relatives'. The more closely we are related to someone, the more genes we will have in common. And by helping a relative and increasing his or her fitness, we actually increase our own fitness.

It was therefore necessary for us to evolve an ability to recognize relatives. This was simple enough. When our instincts for altruism evolved, we existed as small bands of hunter–gatherers or 'tribes'. The members of a tribe would have looked and behaved in a similar way. Everyone in such a small group must be quite closely related. Consequently our instincts evolved to tell us that if we are part of a closely knit group of individuals who are similar to us, we should assume that they are related to us and behave altruistically towards them.

Many of the devices and ploys that are used to get people to co-operate work by 'fooling' people into thinking subconsciously that they are related or a part of the same tribe (which amounts to the same thing). Trade unionists talk about 'brothers' and company proprietors talk about a 'family atmosphere' to imply relationships. Old school ties, masonic rites and company cultures all act to identify people as members of the same 'tribe'.

People don't only co-operate when they think they are related. A second type of co-operation, 'reciprocity', is when someone helps someone else on the understanding that the favour will be returned. Theoreticians can 'prove' that a strategy of 'tit-for-tat' in which you co-operate with others unless they cheat on you is the most advantageous strategy to adopt in life. This applies however only if there are many opportunities to reciprocate (pay back favours). If there aren't, you're better off cheating.

This explains why the conditions in business that foster co-operation are modest levels of staff turnover and small organizations. These are the right conditions – with plenty of opportunities for people to interact and pay back favours – to foster a good game of 'tit-for-tat'.

WHAT CAN WE DO ABOUT IT?

O   Encourage super levels of co-operation and teamwork by creating 'tribes'. To do this, set up groups of similar people on a long-standing basis and allow them to develop powerful tribal symbols by, for example, generating their own customs and norms.

O   But, if you do create tribes, be aware of 'counter-tribalism' – a powerful antipathy to other groups.

O   As an alternative to creating 'tribes', foster an atmosphere where all employees can reciprocate and play 'tit-for-tat'. For this you need a small organization with modest staff turnover.

O   Don't expect instant results. Co-operation can take time to break out.

O   Don't expect multiethnic and multicultural groups to start co-operating as quickly as mono-ethnic groups. But, remember that it can be worth the wait – their diversity of outlook can generate more creativity.

7

AGGRESSION
and how to avoid it

This is probably the most ghastly economic indicator that you will ever come across: a hundred years ago in the American South, as the price of cotton fell, so the number of lynchings would rise. This awful statistic reflects an important feature of human behaviour: as resources become more scarce, people become more aggressive.

But if the purpose of aggression is to procure more resources, in a modern society the exact opposite often results. Studies show that childhood bullies tend to become unsuccessful adults with poor jobs or no job. Unrestrained aggression in an adult is a ticket to the dole queue. All companies and indeed societies apply strong sanctions against physical aggression.

WHY ARE HUMANS SUCH AGGRESSIVE ANIMALS?

Why do we need such strong sanctions against aggression? Two underlying reasons illuminate why we humans are inclined to be particularly aggressive.

The first reason, paradoxically, has to do with the fact that our bodies aren't well equipped for physical aggression. Different animals have different propensities to settle quarrels with a scrap. Some animals seem to resort to conflict at the drop of a hat. In other species the two antagonists weigh each other up and one of them, realizing that it is probably very unlikely to be the victor, adopts some sort of appeasement or subordination display.

111

You may have noticed this in your dog when it rolls over on its back as a larger dog approaches.

What sorts of animals have the most highly developed appeasement and subordination behaviours? It becomes obvious when given some thought: those who have the most to lose from an actual conflict. So carnivorous animals, equipped with vicious teeth and claws, are more reluctant to enter into actual conflict and are more prepared to accept subordinacy on the basis of who would *probably* have won a fight. Hence animals such as dogs and wolves (from whom your dog recently evolved) will adopt the appropriate submissive posture.

Which animals are more prepared to 'have a go'? Those for whom conflict is less likely to cause actual injury. This includes animals without built in weaponry, such as sheep and animals who can, because of their mobility, easily beat a retreat if the conflict doesn't go their way. Take a surprising example, the symbol of peace, the dove. If you cage two doves together, one will readily beat the other to death; there is no adequate submission procedure as in normal conditions the vanquished dove would simply fly away.

Then there are animals that come somewhere in between these two extremes. They are not carrying built-in lethal weaponry, so they are prepared for a tussle but they will emit the appropriate submission displays and admit defeat if it begins to look unlikely that they will win the fight. Humans and our close relative the chimpanzees seem to fall into this category.

Our lack of 'built in weaponry' is, therefore, the first reason we are inclined to be aggressive. (The problem today, of course, is that our technology has suddenly thrust upon us weaponry that is vastly more lethal than the wolf's fangs – from guns to nuclear weapons. They offer no opportunity for a testing of strengths and for the receipt of an act of submission. The combination of an inclination to be aggressive and the ability to kill instantaneously is frightening.)

The second reason for our inclination to be aggressive has to do with the shift our ancestors made from being tree-dwelling fruit-eaters to land-based hunter–gatherers. This shift meant that aggression became a useful way to secure food.

To understand why, think about how cows act when the grass in their field gets scarce. You've never seen them fighting over the stuff have you? The reason is that aggression is not profitable when there are resources spread over a large area and the first to reach them consumes them. It would be pointless for cows to fight over grass in a field. While any two cows chose to fight, the others would be busy eating all the grass. Obviously, the best strategy if you are a cow is to race around the field and gobble as much grass as you can. This type of competition is known as 'scramble competition'. This explains why cows are so good humoured among themselves.

For the same reason, most primates (apes and monkeys) don't war among themselves; they settle disputes by ritualized threat displays. Their food is, for the most part, the fruit of trees, which is spread out over vast areas. It is a question of who can scramble around the trees, eating the fruit, the fastest. Just like the cows they are involved in 'scramble competition'.

Of course, while we were tree-dwelling, fruit-eating apes, it would have been just the same for us. The shift to a carnivorous, hunter–gatherer lifestyle must have begun to change all that. A large kill would have been a valuable prize, well worth fighting for: there was a shift from 'scramble competition' to 'contest competition'. There is evidence from the fossil record that the earliest people fought among themselves: skulls that appear to have been smashed by weapons and so on. And today looking at the few primitive hunter–gatherer societies left, the evidence points to a natural urge to war.

As one of the great sociobiologists, Barash (1981), has pointed out:

> the peaceable, 'noble savage' is largely a myth. . . Even such seemingly unaggressive people as the Eskimos often engage in fierce and often murderous competition, especially before extensive contact with Western Civilisation. Similarly, the unaggressive Bushmen of South Africa used to raid Boer cattle; it seems that now they are unaggressive largely because they have been soundly defeated.

The move from a hunter–gatherer to an agricultural lifestyle must have made it even more worth while fighting. A primitive farm would have represented a family's entire livelihood. It's easy to see why they would fight for it.

PARALLELS IN BUSINESS

At this point it might be worth pausing to consider an interesting aside. You can see a perfect parallel between the evolution of competition in human kind and the evolution of competition in modern industry. Here too there was a shift from 'scramble competition' to 'contest competition'.

In the early days of industrialization, firms were relatively 'nice' to each other. I mean 'nice' in the sense that they didn't tend to 'waste' time and money fighting over whose product is best. This was the 'production era'. The emphasis was on efficiency, producing as many goods as possible as cheaply as possible. Henry Ford, of course, epitomizes this phase. His famous 'any colour you like as long as it's black' shows what scant regard industrialists in the 1920s paid to competition as we know it. The reason was, of course, that in those days demand far outstripped supply. Like our cows, they had no reason to fight. They were in scramble competition: the faster they supplied demand, the more business they got.

In the 1930s and 1940s supply began to catch up with demand. Along came Alfred P. Sloan at General Motors. Sloan is famous for his leadership. His genius was that he realized that the days of scramble competition were ending and he made GM into a 'contest competitor'. He did this because he was, perhaps, the first marketing genius (although 'marketing' hadn't been 'invented' then). Sloan segmented the car market and produced 'a car for everyone'. He fought the competition for every car he sold. He even divisionalised his company to achieve this. As a result GM overtook Ford to become the world's biggest car producer.

For a while, after the Second World War, with the advanced world's industrial capacity vastly diminished, demand again outstripped supply and there was something of a return to scramble competition. The challenge was to build factories to satisfy demand as quickly as possible.

Then, as supply again caught up with demand, what happened? Marketing happened. Companies positioned themselves and their products against each other in an ever more crowded market place. The richer the economy, the more this happens. So, in the USA, the world's biggest marketplace, 'comparative advertising' and 'knocking copy' are now rife.

There is also a parallel between the evolution of competition in human kind and the evolution of competition in individual markets. Here again we see a shift from 'scramble competition' to 'contest competition'.

Consider the following brief description of a typical 'product life cycle' by Malcolm McDonald (1990):

> If a new product is successful at the introductory stage, then gradually repeat purchase grows and spreads and the rate of sales growth increases. At this stage competitors often enter the market and their additional promotional expenditures *further expand the market* [author's italics, i.e., scramble competition]. But no market is infinitely expandable, and eventually the rate of growth slows as the product moves into its maturity stage. Eventually a point is reached where there are too many firms in the market, price *wars break out*, [author's italics] and some firms drop out of the market [contest competition].

THE PROBLEMS WITH AGGRESSION TODAY

We have seen that our lack of inbuilt weaponry and our shift from tree-dwelling fruit eaters to land-dwelling hunter–gatherers have firmly inclined us towards aggression. Societies have had to develop powerful laws and sanctions to prevent our genes goading us into behaviour which was quite appropriate when it evolved but has suddenly become a terrible liability in the modern setting. The sixth Commandment is, you will recall 'Thou shalt not kill.'

Our propensity towards aggression is also wholly inappropriate in modern organizations. So it is that overly aggressive and violent individuals are, among other things, consigned to the dole queue. This is one good reason for the modern business person to understand and control his aggressive tendencies.

There is another good reason. Aggression in our modern circumstances can do more than damage your job prospects. It can kill you. In the late 1950s two doctors, Friedman and Rosenman, noted the link between behaviour and heart problems. They noticed that chairs in the waiting room were getting worn down at the front. From such a bizarre observation came one of the most famous pieces of medical research. So many of their cardiac patients were the highly strung type and they were literally on the edge of their chair waiting for their appointment. This prompted research which led to the definition of the famous 'Type A' personality: impatient, ambitious, competitive, and of course aggressive. 'Type As' contrasted with the so called 'Type Bs', who tended to be patient, relaxed and more readily satisfied. There seemed to be a strong connection between Type A behaviour and heart disease and other stress related illnesses.

Later research has refined these findings. It seems that it is above all *hostility* that puts you at risk of heart disease. One chilling example: a piece of research involved 118 law students taking the Minnesota Multiphasic personality assessment; 30 years later those with the highest hostility ratings were more than four times as likely to have died.

The reasons for the potentially fatal consequences of Type A behaviour are, of course, the same as those for the potentially fatal consequences of stress in general that we saw earlier. Stress and aggression both result in adrenalin. Adrenalin, you will recall, being the 'fight or flight' hormone. It prepares the body for fight (in the case of aggression) by, for example, raising the heart rate and breathing rate to provide the muscles with the extra oxygen that it will require in the fight which the animal is assuming may well ensue. The problem (or rather the improvement) today is that conflicts don't tend to result in fisticuffs. And as we saw for those individuals for whom they do, job prospects are bleak! Furthermore, today our conflicts tend to be complex and long lived. Without any release for aggressive individuals, adrenalin produces an internal sledgehammer, constantly pounding their cardiovascular systems.

CAUSES OF AGGRESSION: PAIN, FRUSTRATION, CROWDING AND SOCIAL TURMOIL

We have established that we are burdened with a propensity for aggression that is hopelessly inappropriate for the modern world. We have also seen that our aggressive tendencies can do fatal damage to our job and our health. Let us now, therefore, look in more depth at the causes of aggression, how they manifest in a business setting and what we can do to control them.

The first and most obvious cause of aggression is pain. It's easy to think why this should be. Pain is a good indicator that you are being attacked and a tendency to do something about it, to fight back, would be advantageous. If you put two rats in a cage and give them both electric shocks, they start to fight.

You will of course be painfully aware that if you arrive at the office with a hangover or an aching tooth, you are unlikely to be your normal convivial self. You are, like our rat, liable to be somewhat 'ratty'.

Another universal cause of aggression is frustration. Frustration is an inability to achieve one's goals. For a simple example, back to the rats. Put a rat on a runway with food at the end and, each time it approaches the food, block its access by interposing a glass screen. Not surprisingly, the rat quickly becomes angry. You can see the evolutionary wisdom in this: frustration in 'the wild' is likely to be caused by other animals and responding aggressively is likely to get the rat what it wants.

In an article from the *Harvard Business Review* (1988), 'Power Failure in Management Circuits', Rosabeth Kanter observed that: 'if organizational power can "enoble", then, recent research shows, organizational powerlessness can (with apologies to Lord Acton) "corrupt".' The sort of powerlessness that Kanter is talking about is an inability to produce results and the corruption manifests as recognizable aggression – turf protection and the like. This now starts to look like simple biology.

A further common cause of aggression in many animals (and this includes humans, but not all animals) is crowding. This is not surprising; if the crowding increases competition for scarce resources then we would expect that there will be more aggression. By way of a gruesome animal example, if you take a cage of rats and start to introduce more and more rats into it, they will become increasingly aggressive to each other. Eventually you will see extreme forms of aggression such as rape and infanticide. This is all too similar to the pattern you see with humans: violent crime involving exactly the same sort of behaviour that we saw in the rats, rape and infanticide and so on, is far more common in large crowded cities. A crowded workplace also engenders hostility and aggression.

I shall remember to my dying day working for a successful company whose success had made it necessary to recruit people at a far faster rate than they could build anything approaching adequate office accommodation. (My own work unit, as well as being pitifully small, also doubled as a corridor!) I remember malcontents marauding about actually brandishing tape measures, and complaining bitterly about their floor space compared to that of their peers. The working environment was bitter and hopelessly unproductive.

Our fourth cause of aggression is the subject matter of a whole chapter – Chapter 8. It concerns hierarchies. A hierarchy is an organization in which some individuals enjoy higher levels of power and therefore receive more resources. (For us this generally means money.) As we shall see, the whole reason for an individual adopting a lower, subordinate status is that there is no point in him fighting battles that he will almost certainly lose; it is better for him to bide his time in the hope that his turn will come when he is bigger, stronger or smarter or when those dominating him get weaker or leave or die.

If you take a well ordered social system and remove the dominant individual, you would expect more aggression. It is worth the subordinates testing whether their turn has come rather than blithely accepting subordinacy again. And this is what happens: if you take a flock of chickens and remove the dominant individuals, there is a great deal of aggression as a new 'pecking order' is established. Human history teaches the same lesson. As was said in medieval times: 'When the king is strong the barons are weak; when the king is weak the barons are strong.'

A parallel in business occurs during takeovers. Stuart Slatter of London Business School has noted the turmoil that ensues in a company once it has been taken over. He has also noted that the more experienced and successful acquirers of companies make establishing control and taking decisive action an absolute priority. This has to be done within no more than six months. One of the great advantages of doing this is that by re-establishing order, people's natural inclination to fight and jostle for position when there is no order is quashed. Left untackled this jostling and infighting can be destructive.

Unfortunately, it is not only during takeovers that the established order breaks down in a company. Companies impose the agonies involved upon themselves all too often. The first thing virtually any new boss does is to reorganize. The reason is obvious enough: he wants to flex his muscles and his own organization is the one bit of the world that he feels he can genuinely control. The world outside (which is what really counts) has a nasty habit of being less co-operative. This is not a new phenomenon. Petrobius Arbiter in AD 65 said: 'I was to learn later in life that we tend to meet any new situation by reorganising; and a wonderful method it can be for creating the illusion of progress while producing confusion, inefficiency and demoralisation.'

All of which explains Robert Townsend's (1985) famous pithy remark: 'Reorganising should be undergone about as often as major surgery. And should be as well planned and as swiftly executed.'

Fighting for position when an established order breaks down can be proposed on a far greater scale even than company takeovers. Countries too tend not to be aggressive – that is, not go to war – when there is an established hierarchy. The nineteenth century was, for example, the most peaceful in history. It was during this century that the 'Pax Britannica' reigned. Britain was so powerful, economically and therefore militarily, that there was no point in any other country challenging the order she imposed. Then, in 1913, German manufacturing output exceeded that of Britain. The world order that the hegemony of Britain had allowed was no longer safe. It has been suggested that the two World Wars were the direct result of jostling for position in a new world order. Clearly the USA emerged as top dog. Indeed with much of the manufacturing base of Europe and Japan destroyed, the USA emerged from the Second World War contributing around half of the world's GNP. The 'Pax Americana' that has followed has made the twentieth century (despite the unprecedented carnage of the two World Wars) relatively light on war. The historian Jack Levy (1983) summed this up:

> the twentieth century ranks below average. War has been under way about half the time, compared to 95 percent of the time in the sixteenth and seventeenth centuries and nearly 80 percent of the time in the eighteenth century; only the nineteenth century ranks lower, with war under way 40 percent of the time.

The introduction of strangers to a social group has the same effect as a breakdown in order. It too leads to a great increase in aggression. The stranger needs to be tested out to establish his position in the hierarchy. Add to this the facts that a stranger increases crowding and (thinking of the last chapter) is viewed as not being a member of the 'tribe' and you can see why animals and humans often reserve their worst aggression for strangers. This explains, in part, why some companies find themselves locked into a seemingly inescapable spiral of high employee turnover. Once working conditions become unpleasant and people start to leave, they rapidly become still more unpleasant as the influx of strangers raises the level of aggression. So more people leave and the spiral continues.

EVERY CLOUD

So far I have treated aggression as though it were an anachronism: a trait from a bygone age with no use today. Perhaps that is overstating the case against aggression. This is because we have placed our emphasis on destructive or violent aggression. I can't see any circumstances where today this is beneficial at an individual level. (Today destruction and violence is only sanctioned at a national level (war) and whilst the biology and psychology of war are fascinating they are well beyond the scope of this book.)

However, aggression can mean much more than physical, violent aggression. Aggression means any action which is harmful to another. As we have seen we have had to outlaw physical aggression with the invention of our awesome weaponry, but aggression remains. Today aggression tends to be intellectual aggression: most notably political and (more interestingly from our point of view) commercial aggression.

There is a thin line between aggression and 'healthy competition'. The thinness of that dividing line is demonstrated by the everyday business language. There is, after all, a rich business jargon borrowed from that most aggressive of professions, the military. To quote from Davidson's *Blood in the Street* (1987):

> That is why it seems natural for a reporter to say, 'The bulls were massacred on Wall Street this week.' That is why investors are said to 'assault' a takeover 'target' or 'fall back' when it fails. Even if we do not consciously recognise it, our speech reveals that investment is the same kind of reality test as a battle.

Healthy competition is no bad thing in business. In fact it may well be the most important thing. Professor Lynn (1991), in the multi-country study into work attitudes that we encountered in Chapter 5, concluded that:

> The single most important result of the study is that the level of competitiveness in a society has emerged as the psychological factor most significantly related to the rate of economic growth

and the level of competitiveness was particularly high in the five 'miracle economies' of South East Asia.

This in a sense affirms the basis of free market capitalism as postulated by Adam Smith in *The Wealth of Nations* over two centuries ago. Smith argued that every person working to further his own advantage, in competition with others doing similar work, is the process through which a society grows prosperous. It holds as true today as it did then.

Recently Michael Porter (1989) has observed in his *The Competitive Advantage of Nations* that countries have strength in industries not where there is a single state cosseted 'National Champion' (like the sclerotic and moribund Philips), but where there is a cluster of vigorously competing national firms (like the enormously successful Japanese consumer electronics industry). One of the most important factors in the success of such clusters of industries is the powerful emotional drive to outdo one's local rivals.

Unleashed aggression is an unrivalled liability for individuals in a modern society. Harnessed and controlled in a thriving free market it is the key to prosperity.

IN SUMMARY

WHAT HAVE WE LEARNT?

Humans are aggressive animals. There are two main reasons for this. The first is that we lack lethal 'inbuilt weaponry' like fangs and claws and so never evolved powerful submission displays as an alternative to fighting. The second is that when we were tree-dwelling fruit eaters there was no point in fighting over such a widely dispersed food supply – the best way to compete with other members of our species was to scramble around the trees gobbling the fruit up faster than they could ('scramble competition'). That changed when we became hunters. It became well worth our while to fight over a rich and concentrated food supply like an animal carcass ('contest competition').

Aggression in the modern world is bad news. Uncontrolled, physical aggression is a ticket to the dole queue. Bottled up, hostile aggression is a ticket to an early grave.

It is a good investment to attempt to understand the main causes of aggression generally and as they apply in business. These are: pain, frustration, crowding, a breakdown in order and the introduction of strangers.

There is a thin line, however, between unhealthy aggression and healthy competition. Harnessed and controlled competition is the key to prosperity.

WHAT CAN WE DO ABOUT IT?

O   Don't let your children grow up to be bullies!

O   If you are constantly bottling up hostile aggression in your work, do something about it, because it is killing you. For example, talk to the people you are having problems with. If all else fails change jobs or companies.

O   Empower your people: put them in a situation where they can produce results. Otherwise you'll have frustration and aggression.

O   Give your people civilised working conditions. Don't let crowding sour the working environment.

O   Reorganize infrequently. When you must reorganize, plan it meticulously and execute it rapidly.

O   Keep turn-over to modest levels.

O   Don't confuse unhealthy aggression (highly destructive) with healthy competition (highly constructive).

8

HIERARCHIES
and how to be a more
enlightened leader
(or follower)

The greatest improvement in the productive powers of labour, and the greater part of the skill, dexterity and judgement with which it is any where directed, or applied, seem to have been the effects of the division of labour.

(Adam Smith, 1776)

This is made possible by the fact that large numbers of people readily submit to being part of an organization. They are controlled (in varying degree according to the type of company) by a hierarchy, company goals and culture. This requires that some people be dominant and others accept being submissive. It also requires that a large number of people conform to common values. This, as we shall see, all comes naturally to humans. And, in that it allows us to coordinate large organizations, it is a great strength. But, as always – and as we shall see – any strength prosecuted too far becomes a weakness.

WHY PEOPLE WANT TO BE DOMINANT

It's not difficult to imagine why any animal would want to be dominant: there is, as you would expect, plenty of evidence to show that dominant animals acquire more of the good things: more territory, more food and hence more mates. They reproduce more; they are fitter. The same has been true of humans for most of our evolutionary history. Most societies have been (and in fact most still are today) polygynous (meaning that men can have more than one wife). Higher status, more dominant males reap more resources (riches) and more wives. They reproduce more and so they are fitter. Our evolution hasn't had a chance to catch up with the sudden arrival of monogamy, as invented by Judaeo–Christian ideology. Our biology still tells us (especially men) that the higher the status we can obtain, the more we are likely to reproduce and it is a relentless driving force in all human life. Nowhere does this manifest itself more clearly than in modern organizations.

Henry Kissinger recognized this when he said 'Power is the ultimate aphrodisiac'. Mikhail Bakunin, the Russian anarchist, was dangerously near the truth when he said that 'To exploit and to govern mean the same thing'. Higher status and power **does** tend to result in more resources (riches).

This is true even in communist countries which supposedly shun 'class divisions'. When Mikhail Gorbachev visited Britain as president of the (still communist) USSR, Mrs Gorbachev took the opportunity to visit Cartier's, where she bought some fabulously expensive diamond jewelry, paying for it with her gold American Express card.

BUT WHY BE SUBMISSIVE?

We've seen the case for why any animal would want to be dominant. But it is equally understandable that no animal would *want* to be subordinate: to have less or no territory; to have less food; to have fewer or often no mates. But in numerous species, including humans, many individuals seem to accept such a situation with very little fuss. Surely this makes no sense? How can such a state of affairs enhance any individual's fitness?

The answer is that the subordinate individual is accepting the 'lesser of two evils'. Once it has been established that someone is more powerful than you are, what is the point in fighting every time there is a conflict of interests: you will almost certainly lose and this will result in your injury, death or being driven out of the group (and for a human this could well mean the same thing). By accepting a subordinate position, you achieve what you would have achieved anyway (i.e., nothing), but without the fight. And, if you bide your time, who knows, your turn might come.

Furthermore, remember that the subordinate individuals will have copies of their genes dispersed throughout their social group. By accepting a subordinate role and assisting in the prosperity of the group, even if they never reproduce themselves, they can at least be of some help to copies of their genes elsewhere.

This inclination to accept a status in an organization, and indeed in life, seems universal. Even in societies which place a high emphasis on equality, there is an unmistakable social pecking order. Take the !Kung [*sic*] bushmen. Despite living a simple life with little differentiation of labour, still there are those who are known as the 'best men' and, just as in more sophisticated societies, men either establish such a position by their mid-thirties, for the !Kung through their prowess in hunting and healing, or accept a lower status for the rest of their lives.

THE BEST PERSON AT *BECOMING* A LEADER IS NOT NECESSARILY THE BEST AT *BEING* A LEADER

In the past, the most dominant individual within a group was to a large extent the one who managed to encourage all the others to accept a subordinate position. He was the best at becoming the leader, not the most effective leader. Needless to say, the tasks that a tribe of early humans would have undertaken were not nearly as complex as those undertaken today by a multinational corporation. The most important task, hunting, was controlled largely through pack instinct (and we'll talk about that in a little while) not necessarily by the cunning or inspiration of a gifted leader.

Today, we assume that things are different. We assume that people become leaders because there are rational reasons why they are the best person for the job and because they can produce the best results. We assume that business is a meritocracy. But is this really the case? Has our biology really been so overridden?

Abundant evidence throws doubt on the concept of meritocracies in business.

In a classic study of supervisors in a furniture factory N. Rosen (1970) switched supervisors at random between various groups of workers. The 'effective' leaders, those who came from the most productive groups to begin with, should have increased productivity when they were moved to the less productive groups. It didn't happen. Rosemary Stewart observed in *The Realities of Management* (1986) that in general the record for transferring 'effective' leaders from one organization to another contains as many failures as successes.

At best it has been suggested that the success of a business depends on a combination of effects of the leader, the rest of the organization and the particular circumstances that they find themselves in, acting as a 'group system'.

At worst, it has been suggested that it is the interplay of forces beyond anyone's control (including the leader's) that determines the success or failure of an enterprise. Proponents of this theory claim that belief in leadership is largely a rationalization reflecting people's desire to believe that we can control events.

Again the record in many ways supports such a view. For example, eight of the ten recipients of the Guardian Young Businessman of the Year award during the 1980s have produced share price performances below the FT-A All-share index since receiving the award. Furthermore, business people are, in practice, largely incapable of accurately predicting and determining their future. When asked to predict their own promotions or job changes, managers have less than a 50 per cent success rate, even looking ahead as little as one year.

What this all suggests is that if business organizations are meritocracies they are imperfect meritocracies: the 'best leaders' generally seem unable consistently to produce top results in varied settings and managers seem unable rationally to predict where their careers will take them. In a meritocracy shouldn't they be able to? But, if merit alone cannot and does not determine who rises to positions of leadership, what else contributes? Could our evolutionary tendencies for establishing dominance and subordination have any bearing?

WHY NOTHING SUCCEEDS LIKE SUCCESS

Studies show that the experience of success early in one's career sets into motion what has been described as a 'success syndrome', creating the motivation and commitment for future successes. Those who on the other hand experience frustration and failure tend to suffer decreasing motivation to succeed and a shift in emphasis away from career success to fulfilment in other areas of life, outside work.

One seven-year study found that as less successful managers' self-confidence declined, so their emphasis on the importance of financial success declined.

You can see where this is leading to. There is strong evidence that rather than pursuing a career to fulfil their aspirations, many people change their aspirations to fit the career that 'happens to them'.

C. Northcote Parkinson recognized this in his wonderful *Parkinson's Law* (1974):

> The man who is denied the opportunity of taking decisions of importance begins to regard as important the decisions he is allowed to take. He becomes fussy about filing, keen on seeing that pencils are sharpened, eager to ensure that the windows are open (or shut) and apt to use two or three different coloured inks.

Why should people accept that if they don't experience success early in their career, they should lower their expectations and accept a lower status in life? It's largely a matter of biology.

Take a small 'born loser' mouse, and put it in a cage with a larger mouse.

The mice will inevitably have skirmishes and the larger one will soon establish itself as dominant. But if you hobble the larger mouse, by tying two of his legs together, then the 'born loser' will win the fights and become dominant. Now what's really surprising is that if you now untie the larger mouse's legs the smaller mouse will continue to win fights and will remain dominant – it has learned to succeed and the larger mouse has learned to fail.

Nothing succeeds like success. In the artificial circumstances of our experiment, the behaviour of our mice looks bizarre. Actually they are behaving quite rationally. It pays an animal who learns early on in life that it is no good at fighting to act submissive: it knows that if it does get into a fight the results could be catastrophic for it. Equally, it pays an animal that learns that it is a good fighter to act dominantly: it knows it can hold its own ground and it wants the fruits of a dominant position.

It seems that humans have similar inclinations. However, when our inclinations to accept dominant or submissive positions evolved, it was based largely on physical prowess producing success in fights. Furthermore, fights had a tendency to go the same way if repeated; luck played a minor role – which is why our mice were happy to continue on the basis of past encounters, even after the larger mouse had been untied.

In the world of business, the link between ability and success is not so clear. Many commentators have noted this: Robert Heller (1989) wrote, 'The second myth of management is that success equals skill'; the ABC of business success is said to be 'Ability, Breaks and Courage' – and the breaks play a big part; John Paul Getty realized this when he explained the secret of his success: 'Rise early, work hard, strike oil'.

But we are 'programmed' to assume that our success is deserved and based on real talent. You now see why a 'success syndrome' develops so readily.

And just as the experience of success early in one's career can start a 'success syndrome', the experience of failure creates a 'failure syndrome'. As Wilson Mizner said of a bankrupt: 'Failure has gone to his head'. To emphasize just how quickly people can become demoralized and lose their self-esteem, consider the following experiment.

Four volunteers are seated around a table. The experimenter informs them that the object of the study is to improve their ability to contribute to a discussion. To assist in this each of the volunteers has in front of him two lights, a red one and a green one. The lights are screened off so that each volunteer can see only his own light. The experimenter explains that each volunteer's contribution will be assessed and when he is making a positive contribution to the discussion his green light will shine; however, when he is not making a positive contribution his red light will shine.

The experiment now begins, but in actual fact the quality of the contribution made by each volunteer is not assessed at all. Instead, one of the volunteers is chosen at random to receive a much greater proportion of green lights than red while the others, no matter how well they contribute, will receive more red lights than green. The results are fascinating. The supposed 'positive contributor' rapidly begins to talk more and with ever greater confidence while the 'negative contributors' become progressively more withdrawn and lacking in confidence. By the end of the study the 'positive contributor' has well and truly established himself as the leader of the group and the others have accepted their role as followers.

Making people feel like 'negative contributors' in business is not difficult. Perform a simplistic strategic analysis and tell them they work in a 'dog' or a 'cash cow'. Just as in the experiment, they'll become 'followers' and take no initiatives. After all, they are bound to know that you don't invest in such businesses; you withdraw from no-hope or mature industries and diversify into bright new ones, don't you?

But, perhaps you want to think twice about this approach. Possibly the classic mature industry was the hamburger store in the US of the 1950s. And then along came McDonalds!

One way that the 'success syndrome' can begin is by people being born into successful families. Such people inherit a baggage of powerful status symbols from money to accent. This launches such people into the 'success syndrome'. François La Rochefoucauld recognized this when he advised: 'To succeed in the world, we do everything we can to appear successful'. It works.

For example, in one study tape recordings of British voices, speaking arbitrary content, were assessed by judges (Giles and Powesland 1975). Those with the prestigious 'received pronunciation' were judged to be the most ambitious, self-confident, intelligent, determined and industrious.

As with most things in business, nothing is ever black and white. It is difficult to see where the 'success syndrome' ends and true talent begins. While there is evidence that successful leaders succeed despite themselves, there is also evidence that some do have extraordinary characteristics, characteristics that you might expect to be selected for in a meritocracy.

For example, in a review of two large studies into the qualities of leaders, David Guest (1987) points out that:

> the evidence indicates that leaders tend to be more intelligent, energetic and flexible than group members, and to display greater alertness, originality, personal integrity and self-confidence. The more recent review also emphasises the tendency for leaders to display higher need for achievement, greater responsibility, task orientation, and goal-directedness.

Or could even all this be due to the 'success syndrome'? Whatever the answer, we will now see that such leaders certainly have biology on their side when they want people to accept and obey them.

ACCEPTING SUBORDINACY

As we have seen, people learn to be subordinate, either because they are untalented or unlucky. And once they have done, they practise being subordinate with great vigour. The presence of a strong inborn urge to obey leaders was demonstrated by a 1974 study across five countries in which workers were asked why they obeyed their superiors. The most common reason was a sense of duty, of necessity for the organization to function properly. The workers were ready to obey a leader out of a sense of legitimacy rather than because of the individual qualities of the leader. Again suggesting that *having a leader* is more important than *having the best leader* for the circumstances (Tannenbaum *et al* 1974).

A classic experiment performed in the early 1960s demonstrated the overwhelming urge people have to obey what they see as a legitimate authority figure. You may well have heard of it. The experimenter, a psychologist, Professor Stanley Milgram (1974), wanted to look into what has become known as the 'Eichmann syndrome'. Adolf Eichmann was the Nazi who had sent millions of Jews to their deaths in concentration camps. When he had been put on trial in Israel for his crimes, he had proffered the famous defence: 'I was only obeying orders.' Today we are overwhelmed with disgust and outrage at the thought of these crimes, and the idea that such a defence has any validity seems utterly unthinkable: no half-decent individual would obey such orders; everyone takes it as read that he or she would never have toed such a line. The defence was, of course, rejected as wholly inadequate and Eichmann was hanged. But Professor Milgram's simple little experiment has done much to shake our confidence that normal decent citizens could never do such a thing.

In the said experiment, an advertisement offered four dollars to any volunteer who would give up an hour of his or her time for a study of memory. When volunteers responded they were told that they would be participating in an experiment to determine to what extent punishment could help learning. The volunteer was to play the part of the teacher and another volunteer was to play the part of learner. The learner sat in another room, strapped to a chair and wired up so that the teacher could administer an electric shock to him every time he answered a question wrongly. With every wrong question the level of the shock was to be increased.

In fact this learner was a 'stooge'. The learning experiment was a sham, designed to throw light not on how people learn, but on the extent to which ordinary people would inflict pain upon the orders of a figure of authority.

The experiment began. Initially there was no sound, no feedback from the learner and the volunteers readily increased the shock levels to the maximum level, way beyond a point marked 'danger 450 volts'.

Then feedback was introduced. The learner would emit screams of pain and pleas to stop the shocks; at higher voltages he would bang on the walls or become ominously silent. Many volunteers became uneasy about administering ever-greater and more dangerous shocks; some started to laugh uncontrollably, and to show signs of great agitation and inner conflict, but when the experimenter, standing over them in his white coat, instructed them calmly and authoritatively to continue, over 60 per cent of them did.

Finally the learner sat next to the volunteer who had to force the learner's hand on to a shock plate in order to administer the potentially lethal shock. Surely the volunteers would not now proceed. (Even Eichmann and Himmler were sick when confronted by the physical reality of their deeds.) But still there were those who would proceed.

Incidentally we usually associate such mindless obedience to authority and cruelty with men. Women, it is held, are more concerned with nurturing life than destroying it. But in the 1970s a similar experiment was performed using real shocks and a puppy as the learner. Despite the pitiful yelps of pain from the puppy, all the female 'teachers' in this study gave the maximum shock level. It appears that the urge to obey may be even stronger than that to nurture and protect.

The propensity to accept a role and a lesser role within a group is demonstrated in people's willingness to accept powers greater than themselves. Belief in magic and religion is almost universal in human societies. From the shaman or medicine man, who often wielded more power than the chief, to modern monotheistic religions adopted mainly by pastoral communities such as the Jews (Judaism and Christianity) and the Arabs (Islam). Today, while formal religion in advanced societies is very much in decline are we not replacing it more and more with the cult of the expert and the cult of the great leader!

In September 1992, the *Sunday Times* published a list of the 50 biggest corporate fallers that had resulted from the then ongoing recession in the west. It also listed their bosses. It read like a who's who of the business stars of the 1980s and included Robert Maxwell, Tiny Rowland, Asil Nadir, Alan Sugar and the Saatchi brothers.

Although such facts constantly tell us that the business greats are mere mortals who often owe their standing, for the most part, far more to luck than judgement, we are always quick to replace the fallen icons with new, as yet untarnished, heroes. Sometimes we will simply overlook evidence that contradicts their 'great man' status.

Take, for example, some of the (self-proclaimed) great leaders of business such as Lee Iacocca or Sir John Harvey-Jones. What I see when I look at the business record of such individuals is people who took over highly cyclical industries at the bottom of their cycles and then presided over them as the cycles turned up. They may also be great business men, but from the evidence of their record (stripping out the effects of the business cycle) it's really rather hard to justify such a view.

It's not only the leaders of our large corporations on whom we confer abilities that reason tells us just aren't there. Consider fund managers. The February 1989 issue of *Money Magazine* contained an assessment of 277 of the best known US stock-based mutual funds (known as unit trusts in the UK). It found that five of the funds had outperformed the S&P 500 index for eight years out of ten. People take this as clear evidence that there is a small cadre of superhuman fund managers with mind-boggling powers of analysis and prediction.

However, the number of funds that one would expect to have outperformed the index for eight of the ten years (assuming that over- and under-performing occurs *purely at random*) is twelve. In other words the fund managers might have been expected to perform better than they did had they employed the 'pin technique'.

Economists are no better. They simply make such a wide range of contrary predictions that one of them is always going to prove to be right. Take stock market declines as forecasters of recessions; there are still always some economists riding that particular hobby horse. Yet, as long ago as 1960 Nobel laureate Paul A. Samuelson made the famous remark that: 'The stock market has called nine of the last five recessions.'

It is imperative that business leaders are aware of the strength of people's inclination to believe in and follow leaders. Writers on management have sensed and noted that underlying the rational process of business, people are acting more basically. As Henry Mintzberg has pointed out:

> In virtually everything he does, the manager's actions are screened by subordinates searching for leadership clues. In answering a request for authorisation, he may encourage or inhibit a subordinate, and even his form of greeting messages (perhaps nonexistent ones) may be read by anxious subordinates.

Much play has been made in recent times over the difference between leadership and management. Leaders pull, managers push; leaders create a vision and are concerned with a goal, managers are concerned with the means or procedures. It has been termed the difference between doing the right thing and doing the thing right. It is now widely accepted that today complex modern businesses need leaders, particularly in times of great change. This is because a single authoritarian manager at the top of an organization cannot possibly have the knowledge and insight to deal with a fast-changing and complex business situation. He or she needs to enlist the co-operation of an entire organization to succeed. As noted by Slatter (1984), in *Corporate Recovery*, 'the presence of a dominant and autocratic chief executive characterises many failing firms'.

Yet, the forces of human biology conspire to convince such executives that they are doing the right thing.

As the great Warren Buffet observed in one of his annual reports (Buffet produces annual reports for his company, Berkshire Hathaway, that read like a fireside chat with a favourite uncle. They are required reading for any keen observer of the human nature in business.)

> My most surprising discovery: the overriding importance in business of the unseen force that we might call 'the institutional imperative'. In business school, I was given no hint of the imperative's existence and I did not intuitively understand it when I entered the business world. I thought then that decent, intelligent and experienced managers would automatically make rational business decisions. But I learned over time that it isn't so. Instead, rationality frequently wilts when the institutional imperative comes into play.
>
> For example: (1) As if governed by Newton's First Law of Motion, an institution will resist any change in its current direction; (2) Just as work expands to fill available time, corporate projects or acquisitions will materialize to soak up available funds; (3) Any business craving of the leader will be quickly supported by detailed rate-of-return and strategic studies prepared by his troops; and (4) The behaviour of peer companies, whether they are expanding, acquiring, setting executive compensation or whatever, will be mindlessly imitated.

President Reagan too has commented in his autobiography on the unwillingness of subordinates to criticize. 'In any top position you risk becoming isolated. People tell you what you want to hear. . . Not many people close to you are willing to say "You're wrong".' (S. Sutherland *Irrationality – The Enemy Within.*)

Beerbohm Tree has remarked: 'The only man who wasn't spoilt by being lionised was Daniel' (S. Sutherland, ibid.).

SIGNS OF STATUS

So, being subordinate comes very naturally to us and it's something we practise with great gusto! Furthermore, if you are going to accept a subordinate position then you are naturally inclined to advertise the fact. The evolutionary wisdom at work seems to go something like this: if you have decided that any attempt at self-betterment is likely to be unsuccessful, then you will want to avoid any possibility of fights; why incur the cost when you expect there to be no payoff?

Similarly, if you have gained a dominant position it's best to advertise this too. It's a far cheaper way of securing the lion's share of the resources than having to fight for them every time.

Communicating your dominance or subordinacy is adaptive all round and all animals with dominance hierarchies have evolved ways of communicating their standing. For example, subordinate wolves will slink about with their tails between their legs while the dominant members of the pack will swagger around with their tails high.

It's sometimes easy to see how these subordination rituals developed. For example you will see a subordinate dog hang his head to remove the threat posed by his teeth. Or animals will mimic aspects of the behaviour of infants of their species, capitalizing on the fact that adults have strong inhibitions against attacking infants. You can see this with mating birds when, to appease the male's agressive tendencies, the female mimics a chick begging for food.

Signals for dominance fall into two types: those used to establish dominance in the first place and those used to advertise that dominance afterwards.

Not surprisingly, the signals to assert dominance often strongly resemble animal threat displays: standing to full height with hands on hips and an expanded chest, generally taking up more space, more gazing and trying to 'stare the other down', a non-smiling, frowning face, touching of others, a low loud voice with greater pitch range, more talking and more interrupting, pointing at others and their property. Whereas signals for advertising dominance tend to show confidence and lack of fear. Industrial psychologists have noted such cues being used in the business setting.

It has been shown that the length of initial gaze and who speaks first at first meetings can be used to predict the informal status in small groups. But the use of sheer dominance alone does not seem to be wholly effective. A combination of dominance and warmth seems to pay off best. Presumably people can accept subordinacy more readily if they expect a degree of charity from the leader. The face, to be dominant must be unsmiling, but the voice can exude dominance and warmth.

Once established as a dominant individual in a hierarchy, many of the signals to assert dominance will be replaced by displays which indicate a lack of fear of others: less gaze (but more when talking) and a more relaxed bearing.

PHYSIQUE AND DOMINANCE

These dominance cues were of course evolved over the millennia, during most of which the ability physically to overcome was the main determinant of dominance. Therefore, some dominance cues exist merely because of the size and nature of your body, without your having to do or establish anything. For example, taller people were more likely to come off better in any aggressive encounter and so it would be a useful rule to accept a submissive role to someone who was taller than you were. The problem is that this cue still operates in us today, even though it is inappropriate.

Michael Argyle (1988) has pointed out the following:

> Height has a considerable effect on others' reactions, especially the height of men. Taller men are more likely to be given jobs in American firms, and get higher starting salaries; those over 6 ft 2 in. received 12 per cent more than those under 6 ft in one study. On the other hand, the actual performance of tall people, as sales men for example, is no greater than that of shorter men. Tall people are more likely to succeed in politics – the taller candidate has usually become president of the USA, and bishops are taller than other clergy in the Church of England. It was found by Wilson (1968) that the estimated height of a visitor to Australia, who was presented briefly to groups of students, varied from 5 ft $8^1/_2$ in. when he was described as a student to 6 ft 3 in. when he was said to be a professor.

Boys from state schools who reach Oxford University are significantly taller than the average as are those from public schools. Women who 'marry up' the social ladder are significantly taller than the average for their original class.

The evidence goes on and on. It may be wise to be wary of taking unconscious account of such inappropriate dominance cues in a modern business.

WHEN DOMINANCE IS NOT IN YOUR BEST INTERESTS

Of course dominance may not always be the best way to achieve your ends. That is after all why submissive individuals act submissively. In an established hierarchy where you are dominant, exploiting your dominant position and demanding what you want is the simplest way of achieving what you want. This is without doubt an effective course of action.

Among equals, where there is no dominance established, or where you are the subordinate, then the use of subordinate behaviour is more likely to get you what you want. It has been shown that the use of submissive cues such as smiling, self-touching and head nodding result in better persuasion and indeed that the adoption of dominant behaviours is counterproductive in persuasion.

This is of paramount interest to sales people (although we all need to persuade and sell our ideas in any business situation) and McMurry has commented: 'It is my conviction that the possessor of an effective sales personality is an habitual 'wooer', an individual who has a compulsive need to win and hold the affection of others.'

THE PACK

So far we have looked at conformity through obedience to leaders. We are, however, not just programmed to conform to the wishes of authority figures, we are also programmed to conform to the views of the majority of our peers. The reason why humans should have evolved a strong tendency to 'go along with the crowd' is easy to understand when you consider that hunting was of overwhelming importance to primitive humans. The need for the hunting party to act decisively as a single, coordinated body was vital to the success of the hunt. It was a matter of life and death to literally 'go with the pack'.

Today this inclination seems just as strong. Perhaps the classic demonstration of just how strong the urge to conform can be was a study by Solomon Asch (1956). This is how his study went. Volunteers are requested for a study in visual perception. Again it's a sham and the one volunteer is surrounded by four stooges who pose as volunteers. The four stooges and the volunteer enter a room and are shown, by an experimenter, a line. Next to the line are three more lines, one is the same length as the first line and the other three are of grossly different lengths. The experimenter now asks them all to identify the line which is the same length as the first. The answer is blatantly obvious. However, the four stooges go first and, incredibly for the real volunteer, they all choose the wrong line and the same wrong line at that. Now it's the subject's turn. What will he do? Amazingly 35 per cent of the subjects agreed with the stooges and chose the line that they had wrongly identified. Humans are seemingly absurdly easy to influence.

Examples of pack instinct abound in the business setting. Probably the most notable examples come in the form of financial bubbles and their close cousins, management fads.

Time and time again financial markets lose contact with reality as a hysterical euphoria among investors takes the price of securities far out of the reach of fundamental value. This has been realized for a long long time, but still the herd insists on repeating its mistakes. Paul Clay of Moody's Investors Service commented in 1928 on 'injurious financial fallacies' that

> first among these fallacies is the new era delusion as typified by the famous dictum 'This is a new era. Statistics of the past don't count.' Every period of great prosperity is considered to be a new era and so much better fortified to give promise of permanence. However, each experience has been that the improvement in commercial and financial methods has ultimately been overcome by credit inflation and business rashness, resulting in another backward movement.

I have a friend who 'got out of' shares in the late 1980s simply on the strength of reading a headline in *The Economist*, 'Growth Forever?'. If even *The Economist* is becoming mindlessly optimistic, he reasoned, we must be ready for a downturn. How right he was.

Some people have made a whole investment strategy out of betting against the pack (and sometimes against their own gut feelings if they are perceptive and honest enough to admit that they feel the pack urge just the same as the others). As an example, James Davidson in the excellent *Blood in the Street* (Davidson and Rees Mogg, 1989) tells of an investment 'experiment' conducted by Sir William Rees Mogg for the London *Sunday Times*. Sir William invented two investors: Mr In, a devotee of the current fads, and Lord Out, a deeply conservative individual, suspicious of the latest fads and obsessed with 'real value'.

Davidson relates the outcome as follows:

> Sir William did his genuine best for both portfolios. He did not buy the silly fashionable stocks for Mr In – there were a lot of dubious flotations at that time, as there usually are – and he did not buy the real duds in decaying industries for Lord Out. The results were interesting. For a year or so Mr In rode the waves of fashion successfully, and his portfolio went ahead of Lord Out's. But as time went on, fashion passed to new areas, and those of the earlier fashionable stocks began to fade. Of course some had to be sold. Lord Out moved ahead, and when Sir William went on to do other work, the antifashionable portfolio showed much the larger profit of the two.

Perhaps the most dramatic example of how the financial community misjudges corporate prospects is the case of IBM. When John Akers became boss of IBM in 1985, 'Big Blue' was the world's favourite stock. It had just posted earnings for the previous year of $6.6 billion on sales of $46 billion. The company had shaken off the anti-trust authorities that had been bedevilling it in the US and Europe and was free to wield its mighty economies of scale and scope. The company confidently predicted revenues of $100 billion by 1990 and $185 billion by 1994. Few disagreed.

But IBM had already sown the seeds of its own destruction by then. IBM became rich selling mainframe computers to corporate clients. Its huge service network and reputation gave it enormous market power. (As the saying used to go: 'nobody got fired for buying IBM'.)

In 1981 it had entered the small but fast growing personal computer market, thus legitimizing PCs for their previously loyal corporate customers. Furthermore, it went to a small software company called Microsoft for its operating system and took out a non-exclusive licence. Thus IBM legitimized PCs and created a standard which other companies were free to copy.

Throughout the 1980s chip, and with it PC, power grew exponentially. In 1990 recession hit the US and by that time cheap, super-powerful PCs (workstations) were obvious alternatives to IBM mainframes for cash-strapped corporate customers. In 1991 and 1992 IBM posted the biggest losses in corporate history.

All this highlights the perils of the pack instinct. As the great nineteenth-century economist William Stanley Jevons said: 'as a general rule, it is foolish to do just what other people are doing, because there are almost sure to be too many people doing the same thing.' Henrik Ibsen went further: 'The minority is always right.'

But it is not in the financial markets alone that the pack instinct misleads otherwise rational people. Business decisions are subject to exactly the same influence.

Every so often there is an unexplained rise in merger acquisition activity as somehow a fad takes hold. This cycle is inevitably followed by a fad for divestment and rationalization. No one has much of an explanation other than the pack instinct.

Hugh Davidson in *Offensive Marketing* (1987) notes that 'Fast growing markets often lure followers into long-term unprofitability'. He cites various examples such as the fruit juice market where the introduction of frozen concentrates sucked in so many unthinking followers that 'Now the dust has settled, it is doubtful whether any of the pure fruit brands have made a cumulative profit in the past five years'.

Davidson calls this manifestation of the pack instinct the 'flock factor'. He explains it thus. 'The psychology of the flock factor is not very clear. One would guess that it stems partly from fear of being left out of a possible bonanza.'

This sort of pack behaviour is not restricted to the emotionally charged financial and marketing types. The white-coated researchers are every inch as susceptible.

Brian J. Ford in his memorable *The Cult of the Expert* (1982) has catalogued numerous examples of seemingly calm intelligent scientists jumping on to bandwagons in fits of pack hysteria. One of his funniest stories concerns the discovery in Russia in 1961 of a new crystalline form of water known as 'polywater'. The discovery started calmly enough with droplets of 'anomalous water' that had a much higher boiling point (150°C) than ordinary water and that froze at −40°C into a glassy solid that was 'not unlike ice'.

Within a decade the pack was in a fervour with seemingly every researcher wanting to be seen to have worked with 'polywater'. Brian J. Ford's account of the story from here follows:

> Within a decade after the first announcement of the new discovery there were over 400 individual research workers engaged on polywater investigations, and their conclusions began to get exciting. Many newspapers reported to an aghast public that it was now being claimed that polywater could spread its polymerised property to other bodies of water, turning them too into a viscous semi-solid. If a drop of the substance came into contact with the human body, for instance, then the water content of that unfortunate individual would turn to jelly and death would instantly follow. The property would then spread on throughout the rest of the world's water, causing a drastic and irreversible change in the properties of our planet's surface, and causing (a favourite expert phrase, this) 'the end of all life as we know it'.

Needless to say eventually (in 1973) it became clear that polywater had never existed. Most of the researchers were merely 'jumping on the bandwagon' and 'resolutely endeavouring to make themselves eminent polywaterists without bothering to pay attention to whether their favourite subject actually existed or not'.

'Pack instinct' is, as we have seen, a powerful force to resist. It always pays to remember the words of the American businessman, David Mahoney, who said that 'If two people agree all the time, one of them is unnecessary'.

IN SUMMARY

WHAT HAVE WE LEARNT?

People readily submit to being part of an organization. This is because while we all want to be dominant we are quite prepared to be subordinate if we can't be.

We have an urge to be dominant because while we were evolving (and to a large extent today) being dominant meant more of the good things in life: more resources and more mates. Our ancestors became dominant mainly by being big and strong. This is why, for example, tallness is a dominance cue for us even today and tall people tend (quite wrongly) to secure the better jobs.

However, if we can't be dominant, we have an urge to be submissive. This urge evolved because there was no point in fighting dominant, bigger, stronger members of our group. Better to bide our time until we are bigger and stronger or to humbly accept that the dominant individuals are related to us and let them get on with hogging all the resources and enjoying all the mates.

But then, being dominant didn't require you to be a canny business leader. It should do today. However, while there is evidence that leaders do tend to be more capable – more intelligent, more flexible, more alert, more original and so forth – there is also ample evidence that they often rise to the top by means other than ability. One such means is luck. And once you've had a lucky break our evolution programmes us and other people to believe (wrongly) that we deserved it, setting in motion a 'success syndrome' that can propel us forward to undeserved heights. Less fortunate individuals – and they may be very talented – can just as easily be sucked into a 'failure syndrome'.

Our urge to be subordinate can lead to horrifying results. Witness Nazi extermination camps staffed with guards 'just following orders'. And while managers can't do that much damage, they will implement the most cruel and crass directives without a great deal of thought. They will also become valueless 'yes men', unable to do anything but agree with their superiors.

We don't only conform with our superiors. We evolved as hunters. The need for the hunting party to act decisively as a single, coordinated body was vital to the success of the hunt. It was a matter of life and death to 'go with the pack'. We still have this powerful urge to go along with our peers and this 'pack instinct' helps explain things like financial bubbles and management fads.

WHAT CAN WE DO ABOUT IT?

- ○ Don't assume that because someone is your boss they are competent!
- ○ Set in motion a 'success syndrome' for your staff. Give them goals they can achieve. Catch them doing something right and watch their confidence grow.
- ○ Don't set in motion a 'failure syndrome' for people by anticipating their failure – such as by telling them that they are managing a 'cash-cow'.
- ○ Fight the immensely strong urge that you have to agree with everything your boss says. (We've already established that he may be an incompetent!)
- ○ Fight the overwhelming urge to comply with an idea just because all your colleagues do.
- ○ Don't allow irrelevant dominance cues, like height, to interfere with *your* management appointments. (But while you're at it, get yourself a pair of platform shoes!)
- ○ If you're trying to lead, combine dominance with warmth. (People are more inclined to let you be dominant if they think you are concerned about them.)

9

COMMUNICATION
and how to sharpen your skills

When you think of communication, you will almost certainly think of language, of verbal communication. And the ability to communicate facts and ideas through language has perhaps proved human kind's major competitive advantage in the struggle for survival. But language often blinds us to the rich and immensely important repertoire of 'non-verbal communication' used by humans. Indeed most people will find it hard to believe that we express emotions and establish personal relationships almost entirely by non-verbal communication – just as apes and monkeys do.

We tend to think that, because we have developed such a powerful tool as speech, other forms of communication have been largely rendered redundant or are vestiges from the past. On the contrary, even if we lacked the ability to talk, we would still, through our non-verbal abilities, have the richest repertoire of communication in the whole animal world. We seem to have a range of between 150 and 200 non-verbal signals. This is over three times as many as most other animals and birds and slightly more than our close relative, the chimpanzee. When used in combination these signs produce a form of communication of staggering complexity.

Of course, it would be an absurd arrogance to suggest that such a complex means of communication can be covered in a single chapter of a book. (Although there are courses on 'presentation skills' which do purport to do it in a few days – as preposterous as learning French in three days.) Nevertheless, there is information regarding non-verbal communication that is worth knowing and this chapter will try to present some of it – and perhaps furnish you with a healthy disrespect for the above mentioned type of course.

LANGUAGE AND ITS LIMITATIONS

We humans actually survived for the vast majority of our existence without any language at all. Exactly when speech did first develop is uncertain; there is no feature on the fossils of early human skulls that can provide evidence of whether its possessor could talk or not. But it's a reasonable guess that language developed some time during the rapid expansion of the human brain – as it ballooned from just over half a litre to about one and a half litres, between two million and half a million years ago.

Humans were complex, social animals long before they developed speech. Communication would have been of vital importance, as it is for most other animals, to allow social co-operation, to allow non-violent solutions to conflict, for mating and so forth. Speech was 'superimposed' very, very recently over all our other means of communication as a means for conveying factual information. It did not really replace non-verbal communication for any other purpose.

While consciously most people may feel that human communication is concerned only with language and the logic that it allows, it is not surprising to find that, at least subconsciously, we must still recognize that non-verbal communication is just as important.

Why else would no company appoint an employee without an interview? All the information pertaining to the individual in question can just as easily (and far more systematically and accurately) be obtained by written applications.Why else would no significant business deals go ahead without a meeting of the parties concerned? Why do companies spend millions on human sales forces when the same information could be conveyed for a fraction of the cost via mail or computer terminals?

The point is that you can't actually tell whether you 'like' someone until you meet him or her, because whether you like someone depends on how you communicate non-verbally with that person. People insist on meeting people and seeing whether they like them, even though functionally the meeting is useless. Job interviews seem to be a case in point.

Meta-analysis (a novel technique which allows data from many different studies with different designs to be 'combined') shows that the ability of interviews to predict performance on the job is consistently so low as to render them virtually useless. The validity of interviews – their ability to predict whether or not an applicant will be any good at a job – can be improved by making them highly structured, so that the interviewer strictly adheres to a prearranged series of questions. In other words, interviews are only useful when they are a verbal version of an application form.In which case why bother?

Why are interviews so useless? There appears to be a strong correlation between how much the interviewer 'likes' the interviewee and whether he or she is appointed to the job. It seems that we place so much emphasis on the communication of emotions and the establishment of a relationship (all of which you will recall occurs through non-verbal channels) that the objective information about the applicant (the stuff you could have gleaned from an application form) is largely forgotten or ignored. Unfortunately, this forgotten, factual information about the candidate actually is quite a good predictor of performance on the job.

ORIGINS OF NON-VERBAL COMMUNICATION

To begin to develop a greater understanding of non-verbal communication, it is best (as it is for most aspects of human behaviour) to consider its evolutionary origins. But, how do we know that much of our non-verbal communication has evolved; that it is largely pre-programmed? Well, we can take animals, deprive them of contact with others of their species, from whom they could learn to communicate, and then see if they have the ability to communicate. For example, take a baby rhesus monkey and remove it from its mother and all others of its kind at birth. Then show it photos of a threatening male rhesus. Without ever having seen a rhesus monkey before, the infant monkey responds by presenting (squatting on all fours and elevating its behind – a sign of submission for rhesus monkeys and most primates).

Clearly we can't do similar experiments on people. But there are two ways that we **can** demonstrate that such communication is inherited. Firstly, many types of expression are the same in every single human culture (for example smiling, laughing and crying) and indeed whole syndromes of behaviour, such as anger and flirting, are essentially similar in all cultures. Furthermore, expressions, like smiling, are even produced by children who are blind from birth and have never seen a smiling face.

Many gestures are also totally, or very nearly, universal in every human society. It's harder to say whether they are innate or whether using them comes naturally or inevitably because of the nature of the human body. For example, beckoning someone towards you is invariably done by bringing your arm towards your body. It's hard to imagine it being otherwise. Similarly, tilting the head on a flat palm for sleeping, and pointing.

But what of the other gestures, the ones that don't derive from the nature of the human body? Where do they come from? Much of our non-verbal communication is a carry over from our primate heritage. In fact our primate origins make us somewhat unique among mammalian carnivores: apart from ourselves, mammalian carnivores nearly all hunt predominantly by smell and much of their non- verbal communication is by smell as well.

As primates, sound and vision are of central importance to us. Many of our facial expressions are remarkably similar to those of our nearest primate relatives: the human 'fearface' is similar to the 'tensemouth' face used by primates to show submission (note the refreshingly self-explanatory jargon used by the zoologists who coined these terms!); the human 'angerface' looks similar to that of the chimpanzee; the human 'cryface' and 'depressed-face' are similar to those of the chimpanzee. Some seem to have evolved from our primate past, from symbols meaning one thing to mean something different. Sub-human primates have a fear-grin that looks very much like a human smile. Our smile possibly evolved from such a fear-grin. Perhaps the use of the fear-grin to show lack of hostility, 'I'm frightened of you so I won't attack you', evolved into more of a 'I won't attack you because I like you'. A smile still carries connotations of submissiveness today: if you watch small children in a nursery, the low rankers will still appease the larger, dominant children with a smile and, as we saw earlier, a non-smiling face is a sign of dominance in humans.

The origin of vocalizations is unclear, although one can hazard educated guesses. For example, when startled mammals tend (sensibly) to adopt a posture which protects the sense organs (which is why eyes are screwed up or you blink when startled) and other delicate parts. One such measure is that the throat is tightened. If you combine a tightened throat with vigorous breathing in and out to prepare for exertion, you can imagine the origins of grunts and groans.

The origin of other patterns of other aspects of non-verbal communication are even more speculative, and perhaps all the more interesting for it. For example, why is it that in virtually all animals, including ourselves, aggressive behaviour is almost always loud? One theory holds that by making more noise the aggressor is exposing him- or herself to greater danger (by attracting possible predators), or is calling the dispute to the attention of others of the species (thus risking loss of status if he or she loses the conflict) and is thereby giving the message 'I really mean it!'

MANAGING YOUR NON-VERBAL COMMUNICATION IN BUSINESS

So far, I hope to have convinced you that non-verbal communication is extremely important to humans and that it is extremely complicated. As a business person, you no doubt want a simple, workable model telling you how to exploit what we know about non-verbal communication. I will try to give you one.But first a word of warning. Non-verbal communication is complex and subtle. Attempts to stage-manage yourself with people can look clumsy, embarrassing and often downright weird. Being yourself is usually the best policy. That said, you may find one or two areas of your life where you can see you really are projecting the wrong messages and a little judicious tinkering with your non-verbal communication might not go amiss.So read on.But please don't take all this **too** seriously.

Analyses of social behaviour (verbal as well as non-verbal) repeatedly highlight two main dimensions: dominant–submissive and friendly–hostile. All attitudes can be mapped out in terms of these two axes; even sexual attraction, which is a special form of friendliness with additional signs like pupil dilation and gazing into each other's eyes. It appears that, for business, you are generally best advised to be positioned with a tendency for friendliness and adapting your degree of dominance as the situation demands: using submissive cues when you are with a boss or trying to persuade a peer and using dominant cues when you are the boss or when you are trying to overpower. Hostility is generally unproductive: you can carry it off if you're the boss, but you'll be even more productive if you can combine dominance with friendliness. When you're trying to sell or persuade friendliness is essential. There is an old Chinese proverb which says: 'A man without a smiling face must not open a shop'.

Let me sum all this up in a simple diagram:

```
                    DOMINANT
                        *
            dubious     *      often
            even for    *      best
            bosses      *
HOSTILE     * * * * * * * * * * * * *    FRIENDLY
            don't       *      best
            end up      *      when
            here!       *      selling, etc
                        *
                    SUBMISSIVE
```

But what evidence is there for my proposition on how you should behave non-verbally, as summed up in this diagram? And, equally importantly, to what extent (if you accept my proposition) can you manage your non-verbal signals to take advantage of this?

Let's look at further evidence that you should, by and large, position yourself as I have indicated.

In a study in 1977 two workers, Dipboye and Wiley, had experienced recruiters decide whether to invite two applicants for a second interview. In actual fact the two applicants provided essentially the same information during the interview. What differed was the way in which they communicated. One of the applicants was decidedly unassertive: he showed signs of submissiveness: avoiding eye contact, speaking in soft tones and of unfriendliness: never volunteering information and often answering simply 'yes' or 'no'. The other individual was moderately assertive; he showed signs of dominance: maintaining good eye contact and speaking in a firm voice and of friendliness: volunteering information and talking openly.

You may not be entirely surprised that the more assertive applicant was more likely to be invited for a second interview: it does sound as though it would be easier to work with him. What may surprise you is that even though, as you will recall, the two applicants provided the same information during the interview, the more assertive individual was judged to have better experience and qualifications than the unassertive individual.

As well as showing you the sort of non-verbal communication that people respond best to, you will again see that people seem to place the interpersonal and emotional information that they obtain from non-verbal communication above the 'factual information' obtained from the spoken words alone. Often the facts are distorted to allow the opinion formed by the non-verbal information to prevail.

People who position themselves in the hostile/submissive quarter of our chart tend to be lonely and rated by others as socially unskilled in life in general, not just in business. Research shows that lonely people tend to look, smile and gesture less and to touch themselves more, protect their bodies more and appear more tense than other people. (You'll also recall that hostility also tends to be a ticket to an early grave. So it does seem an altogether non-productive attitude to adopt.)

As we saw, much of our non-verbal communication is innate. But can we override our natural inclinations? Can we manage the signals that we are sending to others to our advantage? The answer is that, to an extent, we certainly can and we all already do. And we start managing our non-verbal messages quite young: babies start to inhibit their emotional expressions, if there is no one there to see them, at about twelve months.

'Raw emotions' come from centres in the lower brain, the more primitive part of the brain. There are nerves passing directly from these primitive centres for emotion to, for example, the facial muscles. (The facial muscles are the ones that produce our facial expressions.) But there are also nerves passing from the higher brain, the cortex, the part concerned with conscious thought. Lower animals can function, to an extent, without the cortex. If you 'disconnect' a dog's or a cat's cortex, it will continue to eat and fight and engage in sex. This is not true of humans. The conscious part of **our** brain is too tied up in everything we do. So it is with the emotions; there is a constant 'battle' between our 'deep feelings' and the feelings we think we should display in a given situation.

For example, liking or disliking are spontaneous reactions, largely emanating from our primitive lower brain, but we are all adept at managing, through our cortex, the signals of disliking, particularly in social (including business) situations. Researchers have also noted that dominance cues are also very often put on or 'managed' as people try to influence each other. It is necessary to manage the non-verbal signals being emitted in many jobs particularly when a friendly servile image has to be displayed as in the case of, for example, flight attendants.

If you are trying to manage your non-verbal communication, then it is important to note that some channels are more prone to 'leakiness' than others. Leakiness is when a person is trying to project a false emotion or attitude and the true one breaks through. Women are the most prone to emotional leakiness. When it comes to emotion, women have been described as 'externalizers': they are said to feel the effects less and show the effects more than men.

The least leaky channel is the face, perhaps partly because we can all practise our facial expressions in front of mirrors. Even so there are leaks that a skilled observer can detect. As we saw earlier, the facial expression that we portray are determined by a 'playoff' between our deep emotions (emanating from the primitive emotion centres in the lower brain) and our conscious 'thoughts' (emanating from the 'thinking' upper brain, the cortex). The lower brain is quite symmetrical in that it supplies nerves to both sides of the body in equal measure. So a 'genuine emotion' tends to result in a symmetrical facial expression.

If we are to hide our true feelings then our cortex must inhibit the expression that the lower brain is sending to our face and superimpose its own expression – the expression we *think* people ought to see. But, unlike the lower brain the cortex is not symmetrical. It has two distinct halves and each is concerned with quite distinct types of function. The half of the cortex that is specialized for faces is the right side and as (perhaps strangely to you) the right half of the cortex mainly sends nerves to the left side of the body, a false or 'posed' emotion will tend to be more pronounced on the left hand side of the face. Try it next time you're in front of a mirror!

It has also been claimed that during posed emotions there are momentary flashes during which the 'true emotion' breaks through on to the face. Nevertheless, studies have shown that observers find it almost impossible to judge posed emotions on the strength of facial expressions alone. Therefore, if you're attempting to uncover an emotional faker, you're better advised to look at some of the leakier channels.

The body below the neck is much more leaky and presentation skills courses often spend time eliminating the nervous fidgets and so forth that betray nervousness. The voice is also quite leaky. Language being such a recent development, perhaps control of this channel has not had time to develop so well. If you have an emotional state that you want to hide, the best advice might be to sit still and say nothing. Of course, such a strategy won't allow sufficient scope to achieve very much. There is another approach you could try. You can resort to a form of communication which completely eliminates all those leaky, 'below the neck' communications: the telephone.

Telephone communication does, of course, play a large part in most business people's lives. Communicating by telephone is a wholly different communication skill to communicating face to face and it may well suit your personality far better or far worse. Face-to-face communication is overwhelmingly about non-verbal cues. If you need to establish 'a relationship' then a face-to-face encounter is the one to adopt: it has been shown that people like people more when they have spoken to them face to face. However, if you want to put forward a case 'on its merits', then the telephone is the one to plump for.

Studies show that when people negotiate over the telephone, it is invariably the one with the stronger case who wins, whereas when they negotiate face to face, this no longer holds. It seems that the whole business of liking and/or dominating each other interferes too much.

LOOKS

So far we have discussed the way we behave, things that we *do*, but what about *the way we look*? Aristotle said that 'Beauty is a greater recommendation than any letter of introduction'. Surely not for a cold-headed business person? What effect do looks have and to what extent can we or should we manage them?

We're often told that looks are superficial and that 'beauty is only skin deep'. Don't believe it. Looks reach down to the core.

Perhaps one of the most striking examples of the effect of looks comes from the televised debates between Nixon and Kennedy. Nixon, as you will recall, was not blessed in terms of appearance; he was decidedly not fair of face. Kennedy on the other hand looked a charmer. In terms of issues, the debates ended as more or less a dead heat: there was very little change in voter's *attitudes*. However, there was a huge swing in the percentage of voters who said that they would vote for Kennedy – from 44 per cent to 50 per cent. Researchers have attributed this largely to the less favourable impression caused by Nixon's face. It is striking that looks can have such a huge effect, particularly on such a serious issue as the appointment of the world's most powerful person.

It is not surprising then that looks have profound effects in business and in life in general. Michael Argyle gives the following examples in his book *Bodily Communication* (1988):

Attractive individuals of both sexes are more likely to get jobs, and when they get them to be paid more: Quinn, Tabor, and Gordon (1968) found that handsome men were paid on average 18.5 per cent more ($1,809) than 'plain and homely' men; good looking women earned 21 per cent more than plain and homely ones. Attractive people are less likely to be reported for blatant shop lifting, less likely to be found guilty in law courts (unless they used their looks in the crime or in very serious crimes (e.g.Effran 1974)).

Singer (1964) found that attractive female students, especially if they were first born, were given higher grades in classes in an American college. This was not due to greater intelligence. . .

More recently, a 1993 study by Daniel Hamermesh and Jeff Biddle used household surveys in the USA and Canada, which as well as collecting data on earnings also asked the interviewers to rate the appearance of the people they interviewed. The results showed that very attractive men and women earn about five per cent more, even after allowing for factors such as education, than average lookers. Plain women earn five per cent less than average; plain men ten per cent less.

Is it possible to affect one's attractiveness? The cosmetics industry will be relieved to hear that it is, very much so. Grooming, make-up and clothes can have an important bearing and even such drastic measures as plastic surgery can prove worthwhile.

A 1986 'before and after' study of mouth and lower face surgery patients found that not only were people rated as more attractive after the surgery, but also as more intelligent.

On clothes, Michael Argyle (1988) again:

> Molloy (1975; 1977) recommended that ambitious people should 'dress for success', e.g. wear a suit and tie for men, and restrained, dark costumes for women. There is some evidence that this works.In a market research survey Green and Giles (1973) found that wearing a tie produced more compliance, though not with working class people. Forsyth, Drake and Hogan (1985) showed video tapes of a woman 'job applicant' for a middle management position wearing four different outfits which varied in masculinity. Personnel administrators gave much higher ratings on forceful, self-resilient, dynamic, aggressive and decisive to the second most masculine outfit. Harp, Stretch and Harp (1985) found that newscasters were thought more credible and the news was remembered better when they wore conservative rather than trendy or casual clothes, especially for viewers who wore conservative clothes themselves.

Diet too can have important effects on the way that people are perceived. Among other things, different body shapes have been shown to convey the following: fat people are viewed as 'warmer' but also as less independent; muscular people as stronger and more adventurous and thinner people as more tense and nervous. You can intuit biological reasons for much of this. For example, more active people burn more calories and so may tend to be thinner; muscular people are obviously going to be stronger and so forth.

But, in addition to such biological influences, it seems that our judgement of people is strongly influenced, at least as far as first impressions are concerned, by social stereotypes. For example, in one study people were judged to be fourteen IQ points more intelligent when they were wearing glasses as compared to when they were not. But, after being watched in conversation for a few minutes the effect wore off. (If you face a short interview or a short presentation, consider investing in a pair of glasses!)

We have, so far, moved ever further out from the individual: from the effects of his behaviour to the effects of his looks to the effects of his accoutrements. Can the effects of non-verbal communication be felt even more distantly? Let us move away from the communicator to the person he is communicating with (the communicatee?). We saw earlier in this book how touch is a symbol of friendliness. It can be used to elicit co-operation. Several studies have shown the effect that touching a stranger can have. One study showed that if a researcher asked a complete stranger to give money for a telephone call, the stranger was more likely to agree if the researcher in some way touched him. Another study showed that if waitresses made fleeting touch contact with diners in a restaurant, the diners were far more likely to leave a tip.

So, when the 'One Minute Manager' makes great play of touching your subordinate as you administer your 'one minute praisings' and so on, he's probably on to something. Unfortunately, the one minute manager was a man and the effect of touch is greatest when it is a woman touching a man. (I can't propose a satisfactory explanation for this one!)

Let us move still further away from the communicator and away even from the person being communicated with. Let us consider the surroundings in which communication takes place. Can the effects of non-verbal communication be felt this remotely? The evidence suggests that it can. Even the decor of the room that you surround yourself with can have a profound impact on others. A 1956 study by Maslow and Mintz, asked subjects to rate faces seen in one of three rooms: a beautiful room, an average room and an ugly, untidy room. The faces in the beautiful room were rated most highly.

And even the colour that you paint your room can seemingly have strong effects. One can speculate on the evolutionary origin of some colours. Red is the colour of blood and the colour of a flushed face in times of anger and sexual excitement. One can imagine that red might conjure feelings of affection, anger and so on. The following is a list of the moods produced by the various colours. Think of the main moods you require in your office and send for the emulsion:

Colour	Mood
Red	hot, affectionate, angry, defiant, contrary, hostile, full of vitality, excitement, love
Blue	cool, pleasant, leisurely, distant, infinite, secure, transcendent, calm, tender
Yellow	unpleasant, exciting, hostile, cheerful, joyful, jovial
Orange	unpleasant, exciting, disturbed, distressed, defiant, contrary, hostile, stimulating
Purple	depressed, sad, dignified, stately
Green	cool, pleasant, leisurely, in control
Black	sad, intense, anxiety, fear, despondent, dejected, melancholy, unhappy
Brown	sad, not tender, despondent, dejected, melancholy, unhappy, neutral
White	joy, lightness, neutral, cold

(After Argyle, 1988)

It looks like astrology but there does seem to be something very real at work. *Time* reported in 1973 that children tested for IQ in blue, yellow, yellow–green and orange rooms scored twelve points higher than those tested in white, black or brown rooms. They were more friendly and smiled more in the orange room.

G.K. Chesterton commented about fifty years ago that, 'A man does not know what he is saying until he knows what he is not saying'. I hope I've added new meaning to these words of wisdom. You can know exactly what you are saying (and not saying) verbally and still not come close to understanding what you are communicating to others. An appreciation of what your body is saying to others is, as we have seen, vital to survival in the 'business jungle'.

IN SUMMARY

WHAT HAVE WE LEARNT?

When people think of communication, they think only about language. They are wrong to do so. Most of our evolution occurred before we developed language. Language has recently been 'bolted on' to our other means of non-verbal communication. While we use language to communicate factual information, communication concerning emotions and personal relationships is communicated almost exclusively by non-verbal communication.

We have an urge to communicate with people non-verbally. Why else would we insist on interviewing people before we employ them, despite all the evidence that interviews are a useless means of selection. (In fact they are useless precisely because the non-verbal communication blinds us to the facts about whether the person is well qualified for the job.)

We have a huge and complex array of non-verbal signals, but there are just two main dimensions to the signals they send: dominant–submissive and friendly–hostile. In business it seems your best course is to be friendly at all times and to be dominant when you're trying to lead and submissive when you're following or trying to sell.

Our true emotions come from our primitive lower brains. But we can try to override these with our conscious, higher brain. However, we will have varying levels of success. Some emotional displays – those below the neck including the voice – are more 'leaky' (difficult to disguise). Facial expressions are less 'leaky' and are more easy to control. Women are 'externalizers': they generally find it more difficult to disguise their emotions.

Looks are an important means of non-verbal communication and one that we can manage. This is important in business: attractive people get better jobs and higher salaries. Touch too can have a profound effect.

Further afield, even your working environment can serve as a means of communication. Colour in particular can affect mood and performance.

WHAT CAN WE DO ABOUT IT?

O   Do away with interviews, or structure them rigorously so that non-verbal communication doesn't stop you looking for and collecting *relevant* facts about a person's ability to do a job.

O   Don't try to stage-manage your non-verbal communication too self-consciously. We have a huge array of non-verbal cues, and trying to manage them all can look clumsy and weird.

O   Stay friendly at all times and try to become more dominant when you're trying to lead, more submissive when you're trying to persuade or sell.

O   If you want to hide your emotions, stay still and don't talk.

O   Alternatively, use the phone: the best case usually wins a negotiation on the phone; it doesn't in face-to-face situations where all the non-verbal communication interferes.

O   Take your looks, your dress, your diet and your clothes seriously.

O   Use touch to cement relationships.

O   Think about the effect your surroundings – particularly their colour – are having on you and on others.

10

DECEIT
and how to detect it

❖

There's some merit in deceit if you can get away with it. This statement may well make you recoil with horror. Both your upbringing and indeed the modern business ethos with its 'passion for integrity' (incidentally a passion which tends to wax and wane with economic growth and our ability to afford it) have taught you to abhor deceit. No matter how strongly you think you believe that, I am going to suggest that you will still practise deceit. You may even be one of its better exponents: as we shall see the best liars are the ones that don't know they are lying and we'll see why as this chapter progresses.

Deceit is an integral part of human life and an integral part of business life. A recent book by James Patterson, *The Day America Told the Truth* (1991), is based on confidential interviews with 2000 Americans. It revealed that 91 per cent of Americans lie regularly, at home *and at work*.

This is by no means a revelation. During the first century Petronius observed that, 'a man who is always ready to believe what is told him will never do well, especially a business man.'

Why should this be the case?

HUMANS: MASTERS OF DECEIT

The more the individuals of a species co-operate among themselves, the greater the opportunity for, and conversely the danger of, deceit. No animals are more dependent upon co-operation for their survival than humans.

Without the support of a group, a society, we are all but helpless. We've discussed the reasons that people co-operate: through altruism, the helping of copies of our genes sitting inside the bodies of relatives; through 'reciprocity', the 'tit-for-tat' trading of favours; and through the powers of status and conformism that make the functioning of a society possible.

The amount of assistance that we receive from others is determined by their view of us: how related we are to them, what favours we have done or can do for them and what our status in the group is. For most animals this is more straightforward than for us. They can't talk and so each gains an impression of the other by what it observes: the outcomes of fights for dominance; acts of kindness, food sharing and so on. All can be seen for what they are.

That all changed for us once we developed language. False information could be given out very cheaply, simply by talking, by telling lies. Talk, as the old saw has it, is cheap. It's as easy to say 'yes' as it is 'no'. The effort is minimal and the returns can be great. It has even been suggested that the evolution of such a large human brain was stimulated to some extent by the opportunities for practising, and the need to detect, deceit.

Obviously it is in each individual's interests to present an image of him- or herself that generates as much assistance as possible from others. And that is **not** the true image of a ruthlessly selfish individual solely concerned with the propagation of his or her own genes. Ben Jonson seemed to sense this when he said: 'It holds for good policy ever, to have that outwardly in vilest estimation, that inwardly is most dear to us.'

WHY THE BEST LIARS DON'T KNOW THEY'RE LYING: SELF-DECEPTION

Jerome K. Jerome observed that: 'It is always the best policy to speak the truth, unless of course you are an exceptionally good liar.'

We saw in our chapter on communication how emotional leakage can betray our true feelings. When we lie we feel tense and the sweaty palms and shaky voice can be a sure giveaway. What we are saying and the way we are behaving are out of line and our lies may be detected. The best solution is for you not to know that you are lying. Take an example from the world of birds. For many species of bird, the more dominant the bird, the darker its plumage. The dominant birds win first call on food and mates, so why on earth don't the lighter coloured, submissive birds cheat by growing darker plumages themselves? Researchers interested in this question took submissive birds and dyed them darker. The result was that 'liars' who were proclaiming unearned dominance were attacked by the 'real' dominants. The reason that they were attacked was that they were 'saying' with their plumage that they were strong and dominant but they were acting weak and submissive.

Next the researchers not only dyed the plumage of submissive birds darker so that they 'said' they were dominant, they also gave them injections of the male hormone testosterone to make them act dominant. The birds truly believed they were superior and strutted around accordingly. And this time they got away with it! These birds were successful in deceiving other birds because they believed in the deceit themselves.

You can see the evolutionary advantage that there would be if in deceiving others you also deceived your own conscious self. If, when we wanted to deceive others, we could know the real state of affairs 'deep down' but fool ourselves by consciously 'knowing' that the deceit we want to convey is true, what brilliant liars we would make! No sweaty palms, no sideways glances; just a bold-faced, confident, straightforward, unabashed . . . lie. It sounds like supernatural mumbo jumbo. But, it has actually been *proved* that people *do* practise self-deception. Furthermore it has been shown that we do this with reason and to suit (wouldn't you know it) our genes' purposes.

If you wire someone up to a machine to measure something called GSR (this stands for Galvanic Skin Response; it's what lie detectors measure) then their GSR will rise much more when they hear their own voice than when they hear a stranger's. Deep down we have an ability to recognize and respond to ourselves.

Now, recall when we discussed dominance; we learnt that if you are dominant, it pays to advertise it and if you are submissive, it pays to advertise that too. Part of being dominant is projecting yourself more. And as a result successful, dominant people tend to be more 'self-involved' than others: they like to look at themselves in pictures and in mirrors and listen to their own voice more. The more people experience success, the more self-involved they tend to be. It seems that these people like the sound of their own voice so much that, if they are played a series of recorded voices, some of which are their own and some of which belong to other people, they will 'project' themselves and claim to hear themselves not only when their own voice is played, but also for a proportion of the recordings of other people.

Conversely, part of being submissive is maintaining a low profile. So, unsuccessful, submissive people tend to be less 'self-involved': they shy away from mirrors; they don't like the sound of their own voice. In fact, they are so coy that *if* they are played a series of recorded voices, some of which are their own and some of which belong to other people, they will invariably recognize other people's voices as not being their own, but they will also at times deny ownership of their own voice.

So far this seems to belong to our chapter on status; until, that is, we consider what the measurements of the skin's GSR was telling us. It seems that while these subjects were incorrectly projecting or denying the sound of their own voice – and incidentally quite unintentionally as far as they were concerned – their skin, by and large, 'knew' exactly whose voice it was. The GSR rose at the sound of their own voice, and *only* at the sound of their own voice! Thus we have a situation where the unconscious mind is aware of the truth and the conscious mind is made to believe in different and false information at the same time. And, it seems to be acting in people's genes' best interests. (As I said we have already seen why advertising dominance or submissiveness is in genes' best interests.)

In everyday life it seems that self-deception is amazingly common and psychologists have classified various types. As we examine some of these, you will be struck by how often you recognize them in the world of business.

BENEFFECTANCE

We all like to be seen as benevolent towards others and as effective (these encourage 'tit-for-tat' benevolence in our direction – you are likely to be benevolent to others and it's surely better to play 'tit-for-tat' with someone who can be of benefit to you). This combination of benevolence and effectiveness has been dubbed 'beneffectance'. People tend to increase their 'beneffectance' rating by exaggerating their part in a favourable outcome and understating or denying their part in an unfavourable outcome.

You can demonstrate this phenomenon simply and elegantly in an experimental setting. A subject is asked to press one of two buttons. Each time he presses one or the other a sign illuminates to tell him whether he has scored or not. The sign actually lights up at random: the subject has no control over it whatsoever. Nevertheless, the subject will, after a number of presses, come to believe that he has obtained some measure of control over the system.

This is, however, by no means simply a theoretical or experimental phenomenon. Examples are all around you as a business person.

Good business performances tend to have been '*achieved*' and are talked of in the active voice. An example comes from the B.A.T. results statement for the three months to March 1990, which just happens to be in a randomly selected back copy of *The Economist*: 'Tobacco: year started with a strong performance from the group's tobacco businesses . . .'

Business failures, on the other hand, tend to have '*happened*' and are often talked of in the passive voice. Again, from the same B.A.T. statement: 'Exceptional combination of factors at Eagle Star – severe weather underwriting losses and lower stock market values – led to reduction in pre-tax profit.'

I'm not suggesting that B.A.T. is being deceitful in this particular statement, but whenever you look at results statements or annual reports the same pattern emerges. Companies always 'achieve' good results and 'experience' adverse conditions leading to poor results. Have fun browsing through the financial pages and you'll see what I mean.

Another shining example of beneffectance can be seen staring at you from every airport bookshelf, the constant cascade of 'How I Did It' books by today's successful executives. The overwhelming impression is that these people firmly believe that their companies' successes were almost entirely their own doing. Of course, many of these people are hugely talented and contributed greatly to their companies' successes, but market forces, trade cycles and all the uncontrollables that we know full well play an important part are relegated to bit parts or are written out completely. We know, from the evidence for companies' successes being attributable to leaders, from the earlier chapter on conformity, that these other factors are at the very least co-stars in the stories and in many cases they are indisputably *the* stars.

'Beneffectance' is a powerful force in business: you don't see many 'How I Cocked It Up' books.

Corporations employ specialists in 'beneffectance': they are called public relations specialists. Alex Harrington has summed up their role: 'Public relations specialists make flower arrangements of the facts, placing them so that the wilted and less attractive petals are hidden by sturdy blooms', and 'There are a million definitions of public relations. I have found it to be the craft of arranging the truth so that people like you'.

The whole western business community seems to be engaging in a collective act of 'beneffectance' at the moment. So many of our failures are supposedly due to the 'unfair trading practices' of the Japanese. The accusations are never ending: MITI (the Japanese Ministry of International Trade and Industry) is supposed to have some sinister ability to coordinate strategic industries to the detriment of western firms (despite the fact that the industries MITI has actually targeted have generally been failures); the yen is supposed to be held artificially low (despite the fact that there is no conceivable mechanism for this and that the yen appreciated 100 per cent in the mid-1980s); their cost of capital is supposed to be lower than ours (despite the fact that with global capital markets real interest rates and real costs of capital are more or less the same the world over) and so it goes on.

The one thing that is never countenanced is that the Japanese are better managers than we are. The unfortunate truth is that they are. There are, for me, two main reasons: they concentrate on the real working problems of their business rather than abstract strategy techniques; and they concentrate on people. Perhaps reading a book like this might redress the latter a little for some in the west. This would be far more productive than continuing to resort to 'beneffectance'.

Beneffectance is perhaps best summed up in the words of Anthony Sampson: 'We are an indispensable team; you are overmanned; they are redundant.'

An obvious corollary of people overestimating the extent to which they contribute to favourable outcomes in the *past* is that they will be overoptimistic about their prospects for controlling events in the *future.*

As a result, people overvalue what they freely chose: employees at a couple of firms were sold $1 lottery tickets. Some were simply given their tickets, others were allowed to chose their number. The experimenters later tried to buy back the tickets. Those who had had no choice sold their tickets back, on average, for $1.96. Those who had chosen demanded on average $8.67 (E. J. Langer, 1977).

EXAGGERATION

The next type of self-deception is exaggeration. Accomplishments with which we are associated always tend to grow with each retelling. On the other hand it's a fair bet that failures will diminish.

I hope I'm not committing a further outrage by including the Apostles as an example of exaggeration. Still the fact remains that there are inconsistencies between, for example, the testaments according to, say, Mark and Matthew. In several instances Mark and Matthew quantify aspects of their story. Writing earlier than Matthew, Mark talks of the feeding of the four thousand (after which there were seven basketfuls left over). Writing considerably later, no doubt after many retellings, Matthew tells of (you've guessed it) the feeding of the five thousand (after which there were twelve basketfuls).

Still *no one* really got anywhere without a little creative embellishment. As Voltaire put it, 'Exaggeration is the inseparable companion of greatness'.

That only seems to hold for a little while as far as company results are concerned. A 1992 study by Baruch Lev and Ramu Thiagarajan of the University of California at Berkeley, reviewed American firms that used accounting ploys to boost earnings. In the first year after the trick was employed, the share price was not affected. However, over the five years after the trick was deployed, the tricksters' share prices underperformed the market, on average, by 20–25 per cent. By then, however, the managers who had used the accounting ploys had presumably cashed in their share options and been long gone!

Perhaps the executives who massage accounts in this way know only too well that they are exaggerating. Often, business people don't.

The price of pharmaceutical products varies from country to country. This is partly because of exchange rate variation after prices have been set and partly because some countries simply allow higher prices than others. Because of these differences, pharmaceutical companies 'suffer' from what is known as 'parallel imports'. Pharmacists will ship in medicines from 'cheap' countries to sell at higher prices in 'expensive' countries. (By which means they, rather than the pharmaceutical companies, pocket the price differential. It's all quite legal. In fact governments encourage it as a way of keeping costs down.) Pharmaceutical sales are monitored by sales audits which capture the sales of product as they leave wholesalers. This means that if you're a general manager in an 'expensive' country, and your products are parallel imported from a neighbouring 'cheap' country, you are not credited with all the sales you should be. (The sales came out of your neighbour's wholesaler not yours.)

I have seen more than one pharmaceutical company adjusting its market performance figures to take account of parallel imports by adding parallel import sales on to wholesaler sales for each country 'suffering' from parallel imports, so that they should be properly credited with their sales.

This does wonderful things to the market share figures. First, because all of the parallel sales are now recorded not once but twice (once in the country from which they originated and now a second time in the country of destination), and second because the same adjustment has not been performed for the competition, which makes the market share statistics look rosier still.

Of course exaggeration doesn't always work in your best interests.

In the UK there was a great public backlash against the profit bonanzas that the privatized (near) monopoly utility companies like British Telecom and British Gas delivered to their shareholders. This had much to do with exaggeration. These firms used to use 'current cost accounting'. That means that if you bought something two years ago and sold it today, you would deduct the price that you would have to pay for it today when calculating your profit on that sale. This seems a fair thing to do. It gives a fairer view of the profit you are making in today's terms. As soon as they went private, these firms abandoned their current cost accounting and switched to 'historical cost accounting'. This means that, in calculating your profit on a sale, you deduct the price you paid, irrespective of what you would have to pay today. Clearly this boosts your profits. This is a typical bit of business exaggeration (that went wrong).

Business people are not only prone to exaggeration. They are of course subject to it too. A good example is government statistics. Businesses need government statistics on national economies to know how big markets are and plan long-term strategies. Economic success and success of an incumbent government at the polls go hand in hand. Every government longs to bolster the image of his country's economic standing.

Here's an example of how rich countries deceive themselves by exaggerating the size of their national economies and their standing in the league tables of national wealth. The most commonly used GDP figures for developing countries are misleading: they grossly understate their size relative to rich ones. This is because, traditionally, local currency GDPs are converted into dollars at market exchange rates. However, this fails to take into account the fact that the cost of living is much lower in developing countries. In other words, many goods cost considerably less there. The only sensible way to take this into account is to use 'Purchasing Power Parity' exchange rates, which take into account international price differences. On this basis China and India have the second and fourth largest economies in the world and a G7 constituted on this basis would include these countries and exclude Britain and Canada.

This is by no means the only problem with official statistics. Official statistics are, as we know from the frequent revisions, often flawed. Perhaps more worrying is the fact that they are often rigged as well.

The Economist publishes a 'good statistics guide', a ranking of countries according to the accuracy and integrity of its statistics, as perceived by statisticians. Based on the timeliness and small revisions for Britain's statistics, it should come first. However, it comes a poor sixth. The reason is that the statistics aren't trusted. (Of the 30 revisions to the way Britain measures unemployment during the 1980s, all but one decreased the count.)

Perhaps we are being overly generous (or naïve) to include these sorts of exaggerations as a type of self-deception. Britain's statisticians are notoriously 'close' to their ministerial overlords. A recent Eurostat study of the statistical offices of EC members remarked: 'Living under the same roof as an attractive person of the opposite sex can generate impure thoughts. Cohabitation with a ministry . . . can raise problems of independence.'

CREATION OF CONSISTENCY

A close relative to exaggeration is the creation of consistency. George Orwell in his book *1984* gave a good piece of advice to business leaders: 'The secret of rulership is to combine a belief in one's own infallibility with a power to learn from past mistakes.' And over a hundred and fifty years ago Alexis de Tocqueville summed it up beautifully: 'A man finds it almost as difficult to be inconsistent in his language as to be consistent in his conduct.'

People are much more likely to adhere to a decision if they have voiced it publicly. This, of course, in large part, explains the success of organizations like Weight Watchers and Alcoholics Anonymous where participants have to announce to a peer group their intention to slim or quit.

In a classic demonstration of misplaced consistency, a group of

Californian housewives were approached and asked to display a discreet sign outside their homes saying 'Be a safe driver'. Most agreed to do so. Then they and another group of housewives who had not been approached about the first discreet sign were asked to display a very large, ugly sign proclaiming 'Be a safe driver'. Three-quarters of those who had agreed to put up the discreet sign agreed to the erection of the ugly one. Only one in six of the housewives who were being approached for the first time did.

Examples of misplaced consistency are legion in business. In a famous study by Vroom (1966), business students nearing the end of their course had already visited a number of prospective employers. They were asked to rate the three best and generally all three were rated similarly. They were asked to rate them again after they had made their choice on which firm to work for. Despite the fact that they were aware of no new information, they now rated their chosen firm much higher than the others and much higher than they initially rated it themselves.

Sales people can use people's desire for consistency as a powerful lever. If you can persuade a prospect (a potential customer) to commit to buying a basic and cheap version of your product or service, it then becomes relatively easy to 'sell up' and gradually entice them to commit to more extravagant and expensive versions. The process is known as 'the slide'. (An approach that shouldn't really be anything new – it has after all been the basis of seduction for centuries.)

People's desire for consistency has produced some far more dramatic results in business. Particularly when firms and organizations have embarked upon heroic projects and have pressed ahead with them – presumably because of their need for consistency – in the face of overwhelming evidence that the course of action was doomed.

In March 1993, *The Economist* proposed a taxonomy for failures in big engineering projects. Such failures can be categorized as a 'Concorde', a 'Comet' or a 'Spruce Green'.

A 'Concorde' is probably the most common. In this type of failure, it rapidly becomes evident that the project will simply cost too much and take too long to be worthwhile. But, organizations seem to find it nigh on impossible to kill these projects once they are under way. The need for consistency must be a key factor. Other examples would include fitting 'Foxhunter' radars to Tornado aircraft and the Channel Tunnel.

A 'Comet' is rarer. Named after the De Havilland Comet, the first commercial jet aircraft which appeared a great success, until they started dropping out of the sky because of metal fatigue caused by an unseen design fault. In this instance consistency is not a problem.

A 'Spruce Green' is a project that is clearly badly conceived, badly executed and often pointless. It takes its name from Howard Hughes' folie de grandeur – a huge wooden sea plane that was clearly never going to fly –

and apart from one faltering climb to 20 meters didn't. Other examples would include Taurus, the London Stock Exchange's paperless settlement system, which was finally put out of its misery in 1993 after 10 years of meandering design work and millions of wasted money, and EuroDisney, the struggling leisure park. Again, having committed to the project, organizations seem to find it possible to be inconsistent and admit that they were wrong.

Thus two of the three types of key project failure seem to because of a desire for consistency at all costs.

The need for consistency not only drives companies to keep doing senseless things, it also drives them to keep *not* doing sensible things.

AT&T invented the cellular telephone in the 1940s. It, however, saw cellular telephones as never being more than niche products. At the time of its break-up in 1984, it still believed this, forecasting 900 thousand domestic users by the year 2000. By 1993 there were 12 million and sales were soaring.

Perhaps the need for consistency – which implies a failure to make radical change – is even in part responsible for repeatedly, unsuccessful attempts at restructuring floundering behemoths such as IBM and Philips.

SELECTIVE RECALL

Another way that we deceive ourselves as to our worth is in our 'selective recall'. You may recognize the phenomenon if you've ever had a blazing row with your spouse or partner. Suddenly every incident that has occurred since you married and that adds weight to his or her argument is brought into play.

You will be aware of an excellent example of selective recall in business if, during a contested takeover bid, you've ever compared a bid and defence document. The would-be acquirer lists his or her companies' skills and none of the target management's and vice versa.

A further variant is selective seeing. There is a famous experiment in which people were shown glimpses of 'flash cards' with words on them in varying levels of illumination. They were able to see words that they liked in a lower light than words which hold unpleasurable connotations. People are able to 'filter out' things that they don't want to see.

The business people who know about this all too well are, of course, advertisers.

One way that advertisers test their adverts is by producing mock-up magazines, asking members of the public to browse through them and then testing to see which of the adverts were recalled. Adverts are, as you will be aware, occasionally run to try and dissuade people from smoking and these adverts, too, have been tested with the mock-up magazines. The result is that in the later awareness testing non-smokers have a fairly good recall of these adverts. Smokers, however, by and large cannot recall them. They don't want to face up to the harm they know deep down they are doing themselves and their minds simply 'censor' this part of the magazine.

THERE ARE LIMITS TO DECEIT

But for all these pressures for and mechanisms of deceit there are, of course, also constraints. Our genes have evolved to programme us to practise what deceit we can reasonably expect to get away with. So there are checks and balances built into our psyche. The urge to lie and cheat is strongly balanced by a sense of guilt. We evolved as small bands of hunter–gatherers. Extreme untrustworthiness would soon be detected in such close knit little societies and the price of ostracism would be too high to contemplate. We will embellish or conveniently forget when it is convenient, we will be 'economical with the truth', but we will not stretch it too far.

This does not, however, hold true for everyone. Some people are born without these checks and balances. These people are known as psychopaths. In our hunter–gatherer bands psychopathic individuals would have been quickly detected and no doubt driven from the band for their unsociable behaviour. Without the support of a society their future would have been impossible and they would almost certainly have perished. One of the most important features of our huge modern societies, our 'super tribes', is that there is no longer this very close social unit which allows such individuals to be weeded out. Most psychopaths today are cared for in an institution. However, with our larger and much more mobile society, a proportion of these individuals seem to slip through the 'social net'. The results can be catastrophic.

Professor Norman Dixon has observed in his book *Our Own Worst Enemy* (1988):

> They [psychopaths or those possessed of psychopathic tendencies] are strangers to shame, unrestrained by guilt, living by their wits and sometimes ruthlessly aggressive. They may lie and cheat their way through life. If sufficiently clever, sufficiently attractive (until one knows them better) and sufficiently aggressive, they may acquire enormous wealth or power and end up as dictators, presidents, or chairmen of huge multinational companies. They may also end up in jail, or the electric chair or as a charred corpse outside a Berlin bunker . . . it would be nice to have a world devoid of psychopathic leaders . . . this is unlikely to ever come about . . . throughout history the possession of psychopathic traits has proved a useful passport to high office. Men or women who are unfettered

by moral scruples, who are prepared to lie or cheat their way to the top, who can make promises they know they cannot keep and may, in extreme cases, think nothing of assassinating their rivals, have a huge advantage over those held back by notions of fair play.

IN CONCLUSION

In many ways deceit is a part of the fabric of business life. On some levels it is wholly acceptable: the sending of misleading pricing signals to competitors, for example, is a normal part of the curriculum for every business school. On other levels it is wholly unacceptable: falsely filling in an expense claim, for instance. But in between these two extremes is a gulf of grey. We are all, whether we know it or not, deceivers: pure naïve honesty is a trait that would have been weeded out by evolution long ago. In a complex society where information is conveyed by 'cheap talk', reality is constantly being bent as far as individuals feel they can. People do it to different degrees. Some are evidently 'bullshitters'; some manage to appear beacons of integrity. But we are all deceivers. To the less naïve this probably comes as no shock at all. It has been appreciated for a long long time. Bishop Whately wrote over a hundred years ago that, 'honesty is the best policy, but he that acts on that principle is not an honest man'. Writing over two hundred years ago, in a letter to his son, Lord Chesterfield advised, 'Without some dissimulation no business can be carried out at all'. Perhaps now, after a look at the biology of deceit and its implications for business, you may agree with him?

IN SUMMARY

WHAT HAVE WE LEARNT?

Deceit is a part of human life and of business life. The more animals co-operate, the greater the opportunity for deceit. We humans are great co-operators, so we are also great deceivers. This occurs particularly because we can talk. Without language, we could only show good intent at some cost to ourselves – by sharing food, for instance. Talk is much more cheap, we can claim to have good intentions at virtually no cost to ourselves. (Some people think that the need to detect such deceit is why our large brains evolved.)

The best liars don't know they are doing it, because then their bodies don't give away the non-verbal cues associated with the tension of lying. There is experimental evidence that, for this reason, we all deceive ourselves into thinking we are telling the truth when in fact we are not.

This 'self-deceit' takes various forms all of which can be frequently observed in business. *Beneffectance* is our tendency to claim we are more benevolent and effective than we actually are. This is why companies 'achieve' good results and 'experience' bad results. *Exaggeration* is often seen in the ways companies report their financial performance and market share. The *creation of consistency* causes companies to press on with projects that have clearly become doomed. *Selective recall* means that people only see what supports their position on a subject.

There are limits to the level of deceit that people will practise. This is because too much deceit would undermine our ability to co-operate. Hence, we have evolved powerful feelings such as guilt to restrain us. A few people (psychopaths) seem free of guilt. They can be very successful and very dangerous in companies.

WHAT CAN WE DO ABOUT IT?

O   Don't trust anyone entirely – including yourself!

O   Discount people's claimed involvement in successes and suspect they have more to do with failures than they are letting on.

O   Look carefully for exaggeration in the way people express their business results.

O   Don't press on with a doomed project because of your urge to create consistency.

O   Don't trust your memory to recall things that conflict with your position on a subject.

O   Don't work for or with someone with psychopathic inclinations!

11

THE BIOLOGY TRAP
and how to escape from it

❖

The study of human kind and our evolution has shown us much about our nature and how we can be expected to act, both in general and in a business context. We have concentrated mainly on the ways that individuals behave. However, throughout the book you will have seen parallels between biology, evolution and the world of business. This is partly because, wherever possible, we have considered analogies between biology and business as an aid to understanding.

PARALLELS BETWEEN ORGANISMS AND ORGANIZATIONS

But can we now go further than analogies? Can we go as far as to say that there are parallels between the functioning and evolution of organisms and organizations?

In fact, we have now come full circle. For, as we saw at the outset of this book, Charles Darwin originally found the ideas for evolution and the survival of the fittest in the workings of Adam Smith and in the concept of *laissez-faire* economics. Biology and genetics have since become more of a rigorous and testable science than economics or business could ever hope to become. It therefore seems sensible that as business people we should now look to biology for fresh insights.

This is not a new concept. The idea that businesses, or even entire economies, function in ways that parallel living organisms is part of everyday experience if we stop to think about it. Economies are said to 'grow'. Products have a 'life-cycle'.

167

The most eminent of business writers acknowledge the parallel. Peter Drucker, talking about the problems of bigness for a business, says in *The Practice of Management* (1980):

> It is a biological law that the larger an organism grows the greater is the ratio between its mass and its surface, the less exposure to the outside there is for the cells inside. As living organisms grow they have therefore to develop special organs of breathing, perspiration and excretion. It is this law that sets a limit to the size of living organisms, that makes sure that the trees will not grow into the sky; and the business enterprise stands under this as much as any other organism.

There are many other biological laws that seem to have their parallel in business. For example, the long record of evolution clearly shows that two species with the same way of life will not coexist together for very long. One or the other will develop a decisive advantage and the other will be driven to extinction. The need for vigorous antitrust legislation seems to suggest that a similar law might pertain in industry.

The parallels seem endless and these may have to be the subject of another book.

WHY ARE THERE SUCH VARIATIONS IN BEHAVIOUR?

But before we leave this book, I will answer a question which has nagged at many of the people who have been kind enough to read and comment upon early proofs. Having accepted the influence of biology on behaviour, they want to know why two businesses in the same industry, facing the same environment and challenges and both full of people with the same biology, act so differently. Similarly, if biology has a significant influence, they puzzle, why are there such enormous cultural differences across the world? The answer lies in the fact that we humans are in a relatively rare position, biologically speaking.

Generally the individuals of a species are tightly constrained in the way they can behave by the environment. A species occupies a distinct 'niche' in the environment. Behaviour outside tightly defined boundaries is not successful and is selected against. If ants build their nests in a slightly different way it can quickly result in the extinction of the species. So they don't. (Until the environment changes and then they evolve until they again fit tightly into a niche.)

This must have been the case for human kind for most of our evolution. But then, say about ten thousand years ago, our technology gave us such a vast advantage over other animals that we were no longer constrained to a single way of doing things. We achieved what scientists call 'ecological release'. The advantage of using our intelligence and technology in groups meant that a vast range of cultures, even cultures which require some behaviour that is detrimental to our fitness, could survive and prosper.

For example, Orlando Patterson in 1967 described the slave society of Jamaica:

> What marks it out is the astonishing neglect and distortion of almost every one of the basic prerequisites of normal human living. This was a society in which clergymen were 'the most finished debauchees' in the land; in which the institution of marriage was officially condemned among both masters and slaves; in which the family was unthinkable to the vast majority of the population and promiscuity the norm; in which education was seen as an absolute waste of time and teachers shunned like the plague; in which the legal system was quite deliberately a travesty of anything that could be called justice; and in which all forms of refinements, of art, of folkways, were either absent or in a state of total disintegration. Only a small proportion of whites, who monopolized almost all of the fertile land in the island, benefited from the system. And these, no sooner had they secured their fortunes, abandoned the land which the production of their own wealth had made unbearable to live in, for the comforts of the mother country.

Can the same phenomenon be seen in business? It seems that the factors which create enduring success for a business are innovation and economies of scale and scope. Such are the vast advantages to a business once it has established these economies, that it can suffer countless inefficiencies through cultural aberrations and still maintain a competitive advantage.

Given this 'release' there is scope for cultural ideas or memories to evolve in their own right – to a degree independently of the biological evolution of the human species in which they reside. Dawkins has termed these ideas 'memes' (sounds like gene and shares the stem of memory). Memes can evolve much faster than people because they can pass from brain to brain far faster than people can reproduce.

There has of course in the long run to be some form of connection between culture and survival. The Shakers were a religious group that outlawed reproduction. This is the biological equivalent of a company that bans sales. Needless to say, today, the Shakers are virtually extinct.

This is a good demonstration of how this 'release', this freedom to do things in many ways, is not shared in equal measure by all aspects of behaviour. Areas that are trivial, biologically speaking, will experience the greatest and most volatile change. The fastest areas of cultural change are the ways that people dress and speak. For this reason, we have paid little attention to these in this book. Then come political ideologies and business philosophies. These are more stable, but nevertheless change back and forth over time. We've even looked at some of the forces driving management fads and cycles. Finally, there are deep-rooted areas of high biological importance, where there are strong evolutionary pressures at work. These are areas such as sex differences, aggression, co-operation. These are all of fundamental importance to survival. There will, therefore tend to be 'cultural convergence': there will be a tendency for people of all cultures to behave similarly. These aspects of behaviour will be more universal, more generic through geography and time (and that is, of course, why we have concentrated on them in this book).

For an example of how biologically important behaviours manifest, in one way or another, in all societies, consider the following example. Many different societies have and have had maize as a principal supply of food. The trouble with maize, if you have a diet based on it, is that it doesn't contain enough niacin or its precursor (the stuff that it's made from) tryptophan. Without sufficient niacin or tryptophan you succumb to the disease pellagra.

If, however, you treat the maize with alkali and then cook it you increase the amount of tryptophan. Different societies, who have never had the opportunity to pass on this idea to one another have all developed ways of achieving this. Some use ashes to provide the alkali, some lime and some other techniques. They don't know what they are doing or why, but all these cultures have developed this adaptive technique and built it into their culture.

Similarly virtually all companies adapt a results-oriented attitude towards sales. Sales is of crucial importance to the survival of all companies and so there is very much a convergence in the way that companies look at sales.

If, however, you take car parking policies, executive dining facilities policies and so on, there is an enormous divergence in approaches and philosophy. People claim that such things matter enormously. It's all to do with the culture, and culture is vital. If the lesson of biology is anything to go by, the divergence that can be tolerated suggests that these things are not nearly as vital as people like to think.

Of course, an organization can experience 'release' from all adaptive behaviour in some circumstances. Then even the most vital forms of behaviour begin to diverge. Take an army, whose raison d'être is to fight an enemy. Norman Dixon (1988) has summed up what happens when there is no enemy:

> The belated (because counterintuitive) conclusion from peering down the long corridor of martial lunacy [is] that more often than not the presence of an enemy *reduces* rather than *increases* military incompetence . . . The lack of preparation for wintering in the Crimea, for resisting the Japanese invasion of Singapore, or for stemming the German *Blitzkrieg* of 1940 have as their common denominator the simple fact that, when not busy with the foe, maundering and baseless optimism seemed to be the order of the day. Once locked in combat, however, some signs of competence were evident.

The same phenomenon seems to hold for state (and private) monopolies, where hideous inefficiencies become commonplace as memes for non-adaptive behaviour are allowed to take root.

FINALLY

So, having tied up this loose end (I hope) and completed our tour of the lessons of biology for business, let me try and summarize what I hope you have gleaned. At least, I hope that this book has contributed to your 'liberal arts' education as a manager. Even if you feel that none of the detail is valid or applicable, I hope that you will see the people you work with in a new light. I hope you will be a more people-oriented business person. Norman Parkinson has, commenting on the success of Japanese business, noted that Japanese managers are, in their strategic focus, people-oriented rather than financially oriented. I believe that in large part this explains their success. I hope that if this book has achieved nothing else, it has swung your strategic axis round a little in the direction of your people. (Of course the very fact that you are reading this book means that you are already more people oriented than most.)

At best, I hope that this book will allow you to change the way you work.

I hope that you will remember that the human stress response was designed to deal with sudden emergencies. It's fine for dealing with an impending snake attack, when fast, narrow decision making is required. It's not so good for dealing with complex business decisions where in-depth lateral thinking is required. Make sure there are times when you and your people are relaxed enough to think freely.

I hope that you will be excited by your understanding of the mind's unique ability for flashes of insight and brilliance. I hope you will be wary of the traps that can prevent you and your organization capitalizing on these, particularly entrenched habits.

I hope that you will develop an enlightened attitude to learning (and therefore teaching and managing). Remember that if someone turns in a poor performance they will tend to do it better next time if you shout at them. But this is because of 'regression to the mean', not because you shout at them. You are actually dragging down their average performance. Remember too that while people tend to remember and repeat things they enjoy and forget and avoid things they dislike, we don't have a general ('carrot and stick') ability to learn and *nobody* understands what does work best. Stay open minded.

I hope that you now agree that men and women can be equal without being identical. I hope you are wary of some of the excesses of 'natural' male tendencies and that you appreciate that to a large extent both sexes need, in business, to be more like the other.

I hope that you appreciate that co-operation is human kind's greatest asset: 'not fallen angels but risen apes, getting better!' Remember that 'tit-for-tat' is the main basis for human co-operation and that the more the same people work together, the more they are inclined to play 'tit-for-tat'.

I hope that you remember that while, by nature, humans are aggressive animals, aggression in the workplace is a ticket to the unskilled labour market and an early grave. Remember too the main causes of unproductive aggression, like crowding, frustration and, above all, a break down in order.

I hope you remember that we have a natural tendency to operate as part of a hierarchy and a culture. This leads to the 'success syndrome' and the 'failure syndrome' in people who experience success or failure early in life. It is not necessarily valid. Remember too that the 'pack instinct' is a natural inclination. Financial bubbles and management fads are largely explained by this. **You** don't have to be a slave to this instinct.

I hope you remember that we survived for most of our history without language and that we still rely mainly on non-verbal communication for all emotional communication – especially when it comes to deciding whether we like people or not. Remember our little model on how to position yourself with respect to non-verbal communication: tend towards dominance and friendliness, but become more submissive when you're selling or persuading. Avoid a hostile and submissive position on all counts.

Finally, beware! Humans are masters of deceit and the best liars don't know they are lying. Business is full of deceit. Be prepared particularly for 'beneffectance' (and how businesses 'achieve' good results and 'experience' bad results), exaggeration, the creation of consistency and selective recall. Note too that for normal people guilt will limit the degree of deceit. Beware the psychopath who has no guilt.

RECOMMENDED READING

BIOLOGY

Barash, D. (1981), *Sociobiology*, London: Fontana. An excellent popular account of sociobiology.

Darwin, C. (1978), *The Vogage of Charles Darwin*, London: Ariel. Edited and annotated for an easy and fascinating read if you want to hear from the man who started it all.

Dawkins, R. (1976), *The Selfish Gene*, Oxford: Oxford University Press. The classic that first fired so much popular interest in evolution. Dawkins' powers of reason and communication are intoxicating.

Dawkins, R. (1988), *The Blind Watchmaker*, London: Penguin. By far the best popular guide to the mechanisms of evolution.

Dixon, N. (1988), *Our Own Worst Enemy*, London: Futura. An inspiring review of the damage that our biology can wreak.

Diamond, J. (1992), *The Rise and Fall of the Third Chimpanzee*, London: Vintage. An excellent review of where we came from and where we could easily end up as a result of our biological inheritance.

Eiweley, L. (1959), *The Immense Journey*, New York: Random House. A gushing, romantic and highly personal view of evolution. Superb.

Gould, S. J. (1988), *Time's Arrow, Time's Cycle*, London: Pelican. It's hard to appreciate evolution without coming to terms with the time scales involved. This is a fascinating look at time and how different cultures have viewed it.

Maynard Smith, J. (1993), *Did Darwin Get It Right?*, London: Penguin.

173

Superb update on evolution from one of the great names in evolutionary biology.

Shapiro, R. (1988), *Origins*, London: Pelican. Fascinating read if you want to go right back to the very beginning of life.

Sutherland, S. (1992), *Irrationality – The Enemy Within*, London: Constable. The best review, from a psychologist's perspective, of the foibles of the mind.

Wilson, E. O. (1980), *Sociobiology*, Cambridge, Massachusetts: Belknap Press of Harvard University Press. The seminal work in explaining animal behaviour from an evolutionary perspective.

Wright, R. (1994), *The Moral Animal*, New York: Pantheon. A great popular account of evolutionary psychology. Uses Darwin's life as an example of someone following their evolutionary 'programming'.

Young, J. Z. (1979), *An Introduction to the Study of Man*, Oxford: Oxford University Press. Classic overview of human biology. The first and still the best attempt at pulling it all together. Not a light read.

BUSINESS

Begg, D., Fischer, S. and Dornbusch, R. (1987), *Economics*, Maidenhead: McGraw-Hill. The standard text if you want to read more about some of the economics – such as game theory – covered in this book.

Brearly, R. and Myers, S. (1988), *Principles of Corporate Finance*, Singapore: McGraw-Hill. The standard text if you want to read more about some of the finance – such as the measurement of risk in investments – covered in this book.

Handy, C. (1985), *Gods of Management*, London: Pan. A great read if you want to have your thinking on organizational cultures stimulated further.

Hunt, J. W. (1986), *Managing People at Work*, Maidenhead: McGraw-Hill. A fascinating review to stimulate further your thinking on managing and organizing people.

Miller, D. (1990), *The Icarus Paradox*, New York: Harper Business. If you want to learn more about the way habitual ways of doing things can lead to failure, this book is a must. Case after case of once successful companies failing because they couldn't stop doing what used to be a good idea.

Naisbitt, N. and Aburdene, P. (1990), *Mega-Trends 2000*, London: Sidgwick and Jackson. Wonderful statistics and thoughts on how the world is changing. The section on the sexes adds neatly to the information here.

Parkinson, C. N. (1974), *Parkinson's Law or The Pursuit of Progress*, Harmondsworth: Penguin. Some tongue-in-cheek thoughts on organizational malaise. Much of which will ring a bell after this read.

Parkinson, C. N., Rustomji, M. K. and Sapre, S. A. (1986), *The Incredible*

Japanese, Singapore: Federal. A fascinating read that builds on the comments on Japanese culture here.

Rothschild, M. (1992), *Bionomics – The Inevitability of Capitalism*, London: Futura. An enthralling read that draws on parallels between biology and economics to vindicate free-market thinking.

REFERENCES

❖

Adams, Walter and Brock, James W. (1986), *The Bigness Complex: Industry, Labour and Government in the American Economy*, New York: Pantheon.

Alexander, R. D. (1979), 'Evolution and culture' in Changon, N. and Irons, W. (eds) *Evolutionary Biology and Human Social Behaviour*, Massachusetts: Duxbury.

Argyle, M. (1988), *Bodily Communication*, London: Methuen.

Asch, S. E. (1956), 'Studies of Independence and Conformity: a minority of one against a unanimous majority,' *Psychological Monographs*, 70, 9.

Axelrod, R. (1984), *The Evolution of Cooperation*, New York: Basic Books, Inc.

Barash, D. (1981), *Sociobiology*, London: Fontana.

Bouchard, T. J. (1984), 'Twins reared together and apart: what they tell us about human diversity' in Fox, S. W. (ed), *Individuality and Determinism*, New York: Plenum.

Broadbent, Donald (1987), 'Skill and workload' in Warr, Peter (ed), *Psychology at Work*, Harmondsworth: Penguin.

Burke, J. (1989), *The Management of Luck*, London: Macdonald.

Cohen, J. M and M. J. (1980), *Dictionary of Modern Quotations*, London: Penguin.

Davidson, H. (1987), *Offensive Marketing*, second edition, Aldershot: Gower.

Davidson, J. and Rees Mogg, W. (1989), *Blood In The Street*, London: Sidgwick and Jackson.

Dawkins, R. (1976), *The Selfish Gene*, Oxford: Oxford University Press.

Dipboye, R. L. and Wiley, J. W. (1977), 'Reactions of college recruiters to interviewee sex and self presentation style', *Journal of Vocational Behaviour*, 10, 1–12.

Dixon, N. (1988), *Our Own Worst Enemy*, London: Futura.

Drucker, Peter F. (1980), *The Practice of Management*, London: Pan.

Drucker, P. (1986), *Innovation and Entrepreneurship*, London: Pan.

Economist, The, 'The cracks in quality', April 8th, 1992.

Ford, B. (1982), *The Cult of the Expert*, London: Hamish Hamilton.

Fortune, 'Who needs a boss?', May 7, 1990.

Gencen, H. (1989), *Managing*, London: Grafton.

Giles, H. and Powesland, P. F. (1975), *Speech Style and Social Evaluation*, London: Academic Press.

Glucksberg, S. (1962), 'The influence of strength of drive on functional fixedness and perceptual recognition,' *Journal of Experimental Psychology*, 63, 36–41.

Goold, M. and Campbell, A. (1990), *Strategies and Styles*, Oxford: Blackwell.

Guest, D. E. (1987), 'Leadership and management,' in Warr, Peter (ed), *Psychology at Work*, Harmondsworth: Penguin.

Hamilton, W. D. (1964), 'The genetical evolution of social behaviour,' *Journal of Theoretical Biology*, 7, 1–52.

Handy, C. (1989), *The Age of Unreason*, London: Business Books Ltd.

Hardin, Garrett (1972), 'Population skeletons in the environmental closet', *Bulletin of the Atomic Scientists*, 28 (6) (June), 37–41.

Harvey-Jones, J. (1989), *Making It Happen*, Glasgow: Fontana.

Heller, R. (1989), *The Best of Robert Heller*, London: Sidgwick and Jackson.

Higgins, E. T., Rholes, W. S. and Jones, C. R. (1977), 'Category accessibility and impression formation,' *Journal of Experimental Social Psychology*, 13, 141–154.

Hofstede, Geert (1980), 'Motivation, leadership and organization: do American theories apply abroad?', *Organizational Dynamics*, Summer, 42–63.

Hughs, C. (1960), *An Eskimo Village in the Modern World*, Ithaca: Cornell University Press.

Kanter, Rosabeth Moss (1988), 'Power failure in management circuits' in Levinson, Harry (ed), *Designing and Managing Your Career. Advice from the Harvard Business Review*, Boston: Harvard Business School Press.

Kotter, John and Heskett, James (1992), *Corporate Culture and Performance*, New York: Free Press.

Langer, E. J. (1977), 'The psychology of choice,' *Journal for the Theory of Social Behaviour*, 7, 185–208.

Levy, Jack S. (1983), *War in the Modern Great Power System, 1495–1975*, Lexington, Kentucky: University Press of Kentucky.

Lynn, R. (1991), *The Secret of the Miracle Economy*, London: Social Affairs Unit.

McDonald, M. (1990), *Marketing Plans*, Oxford: Heinemann.

Marmot, M.G. et al (1991), 'Health inequalities among British civil servants: The Whitehall Study II', *Lancet*, 337 (8754): 1387–93, June 8.

Maslow, A. and Mintz, N. (1956), 'Effects of Esthetic Surroundings I: Initial effects of three esthetic conditions upon perceiving "energy" and "well being" in faces', *Journal of Psychology*, 41, 247–54.

Masner, M. (1989), *Business Quotations*, London: Pan.

Milgram, S. (1974), *Obedience to Authority: An Experimental View*, New York: Harper and Row.

Nicholson, N. (1987), 'Work-role transitions,' in Warr, Peter (ed), *Psychology at Work*, Harmondsworth: Penguin.

Ohmae, Kenichi (1982), *The Mind of the Strategist*, New York: McGraw-Hill.

Patterson, James (1981), *The Day America Told the Truth* reviewed in the *Independent* 30/4/91.

Patterson, Orlando (1967), *The Sociology of Slavery: An Analysis of the Origin, Development and Structure of Negro Slave Society in Jamaica*, Cranbury, N. J.: Fairleigh Dickinson University Press.

Peters, J. and Waterman, K. (1981), *In Search of Exellence*, London: Pan.

Pfeffer, Jeffery (1992), *Managing with Power*, Boston: Harvard Business School Press.

Porter, M. E. (1980), *Competitive Strategy*, New York: Free Press.

Porter, Michael E. (1989), *The Competitive Advantage of Nations*, New York: Free Press.

Ries, A. and Trout, J. (1981), *Positioning – The Battle for Your Mind*, p. 20 and p. 54, New York: McGraw-Hill.

Rosen, N. (1970), *Leadership Change and Work Group Dynamics*, London: Staples Press.

Schelling, Thomas, C. (1960), *The Strategy of Conflict*, Cambridge, Mass.: Harvard University Press.

Sedgwick, Adam (1860), reviewing 'The Origin of Species' cited in: Tomkins, Stephen (1984), *The Origins of Mankind*, Cambridge: Cambridge University Press.

Slatter, S. (1984), *Corporate Recovery*, London: Penguin.

Sloan, A. P. (1967), *My Years With General Motors*, London: Pan.

Smith, Adam (1937 edn), *The Wealth of Nations*, New York: Random House.

Stewart, R. (1986), *The Reality of Management*, Reading: Pan.

Sutherland, S. (1992), *Irrationality – The Enemy Within*, London: Constable.

Tannenbaum, A. S., Kaucic, B., Rosner, M., Vianello, M. and Weiser, G. (1974), *Hierarchy in Organisations*, San Francisco, Calif.: Jossey-Bass.

Townsend, R. (1985), *Further Up The Organisation*, London: Michael Joseph.

Tripp, Rhoda Thomas (1976), *The International Thesaurus of Quotations*, Harmondsworth: Penguin.

Turla, P. and Hawkins, K. (1987), *Time Management*, London: Grafton.

Vroom, V. H. (1966), 'Organizational Choice: a study of pre- and post-decision processes', *Organisational Behaviour and Human Performance*, 1, 212–225.

Warr, P. (ed.) (1987), *Psychology at Work*, Harmondsworth: Pelican.

Watson, Warren et al (1993), 'Cultural diversity's impact on interaction process and performance', *Academy of Management Journal*, Vol 16, No 3.

INDEX

181